Practicing
Anthropology
in the South

Practicing Anthropology in the South

Edited by James M. Tim Wallace

Southern Anthropological Society Proceedings, No. 30

Michael V. Angrosino, Series Editor

The University of Georgia Press

Athens and London

Southern Anthropological Society

Founded 1966

Published by the University of Georgia Press
Athens, Georgia 30602
© 1997 by the Southern Anthropological Society
All rights reserved
Set in 11 on 13 Times by Books International, Inc.
Printed and bound by Braun-Brumfield, Inc.
The paper in this book meets the guidelines for
permanence and durability of the Committee on
Production Guidelines for Book Longevity of the
Council on Library Resources.

Printed in the United States of America
01   00   99   98   97   C   5   4   3   2   1
01   00   99   98   97   P   5   4   3   2   1

Library of Congress Cataloging in Publication Data
Wallace, James M. Tim, ed.
    Practicing anthropology in the South /
    James M. Tim Wallace, editor.
        p.   cm. — (Southern Anthropological Society proceedings ;
    no. 30)
    Includes bibliographical references.
    ISBN 0-8203-1860-4 (alk. paper).—ISBN 0-8203-1861-2
(pbk.: alk. paper)
    1. Applied anthropology—Southern States—Congresses.
I. Title.   II. Series.
GN397.7.U6W35 1997
301—dc20   96-10267

British Library Cataloging in Publication Data available

Contents

Practicing
Anthropology
in the South

Introduction: Putting Anthropology into Practice in the 1990s

James M. Tim Wallace

The last generation has seen major changes in the institutional structure of applied anthropology. The early 1970s saw the beginning of the
downturn in the job market for academic anthropology Ph.D.'s. Twenty-
five years ago, the principal applied anthropology text book was George
Foster's *Applied Anthropology* (1969), and the most widely used case
book for accessible examples of anthropological practice outside the
classroom was still Spicer's *Human Problems in Technological Change*
(1965), originally published in 1952. The focus was primarily on community and international development.

In 1975, *Do Applied Anthropologists Apply Anthropology?* was the
title of the volume from the key symposium of the annual meeting of the
Southern Anthropological Society. Michael Angrosino was the organizer
and the editor of the volume (Angrosino 1976b). This book was important for me when I began to teach a course in applied anthropology. The
articles in the book were very helpful in getting students (and me) to
understand modern, applied anthropology (Angrosino 1976a). Like the
contributions to that volume, the essays in this 1995 volume continue
to address the issue of how sociocultural anthropologists are putting
their anthropological training into practice. Nevertheless, they also illustrate how the nature of these activities has changed in the intervening
generation.

CHANGE IN THE FIFTH SUBDISCIPLINE

Since the 1970s, Ph.D. anthropologists have been moving more frequently into jobs outside universities, and the so-called "fifth sub-

discipline" has been changing to keep pace. One very important change since 1975 is the organization of a second national professional organization concerned with the practice and application of anthropology. The older is the Society for Applied Anthropology (SfAA), founded in 1941, but the National Association for the Practice of Anthropology (NAPA) was founded in 1983 as a unit of the reorganized American Anthropological Association. The memberships of the two institutions overlap; however, SfAA is not a unit of the American Anthropological Association (AAA) and has its own separate journal (*Human Organization*), newsletter, and annual meeting. The journal most closely associated with NAPA, *Practicing Anthropology,* was started in 1978 by SfAA members at the University of South Florida as a medium by which information about employment opportunities and communication among practitioners might be enhanced (Kushner 1994:188). NAPA also publishes one or two anthologies a year (under the auspices of the AAA) on topics related to the practice of anthropology in the broadest sense.

Applied anthropology is now frequently referred to as the fifth field or subdiscipline of anthropology, given its cross-disciplinary tradition and a re-emphasis on practice. A new term, "practicing anthropology," has emerged to complement the more traditional designation "applied anthropology." Both are now in common usage, but the former has a slightly different meaning, since it can also be used to refer more generally to what anthropologists do in any setting. A NAPA membership brochure describes a practicing anthropologist as "a professionally trained individual who applies specialized knowledge, skills and experience to problem-solving in any of the human dimensions (past, present, and future)" (NAPA 1990, quoted in Baba 1994:174). Anthropologists working in academic settings are "practicing" anthropology as much as those working in nonacademic settings; as a result, use of this term helps deflect attention away from the debate about the value of applied work by those colleagues who find applied anthropology distasteful and want to relegate it to second-class status.

Another change in the fifth subdiscipline since 1975 has been the appearance of new texts, the development of practicing internship programs, and NAPA-sponsored mentorship relationships. The new texts in applied anthropology, such as those by van Willigen in 1986, now in its second edition (1993), Chambers (1989), the second edition of the Eddy and Partridge anthology (1987), and the excellent case book by

Wulff and Fiske (1987), are all helping to integrate thinking about the field and, along with the new journal *Practicing Anthropology,* are helping to communicate new opportunities for applying anthropology.

GOALS OF THE 1995 SAS SYMPOSIUM

Given the many changes since 1975, it seemed appropriate to organize a new SAS key symposium devoted to applied anthropology a generation later, to see what has happened in the interval between 1975 and 1995. The overall goal was to see whether the issues raised in 1975, as well as the answer to the question Angrosino posed in 1975, were the same or different in 1995. Another goal was to present papers that would illustrate the vitality and range of practicing anthropology in the 1990s, especially in the southern United States.

Rather than focusing on products of their research work, the essays in this volume focus on the activities and processes associated with developing practical skills and applying them to the settings in which anthropologists work. Six of the authors work in nonuniversity settings, two work in nonanthropology department research settings, ten of the authors are in anthropology or combined anthropology and sociology departments, and two are undergraduate students. One of the authors also is a medical doctor.

SAS organized the symposium on two main principles. First, all the authors were asked to focus on the practice of anthropology; they were to concentrate on what they actually did as anthropologists rather than on the results or products of their activities. Second, all the authors had to be employed in either an academic or nonacademic setting in the southern United States, or the subject of their work activities had to be in the South. The Southern Anthropological Society is the oldest, and many believe, the premier regional anthropological society in the United States. Its members have participated in the changes in applied anthropology during the last twenty years. Also, many of the best applied anthropology programs in the United States have been nurtured in southern institutions. The program at the University of Kentucky is one of the oldest in the nation, and it and the one at the University of Florida were given additional resources and emphasis. The University of South Florida in Tampa became the first program with a Ph.D. in applied anthropology. Very successful applied anthropology M.A. programs were developed at the University of Memphis and Georgia State University. A highly regarded undergraduate applied concentration was developed at Appalachian State University in Boone, North Carolina. These are but a few of the new applied anthropology programs at southern institutions.

In seeking symposium participants, I looked for anthropologists who would provide an interesting perspective about their anthropological practice. There was no attempt to include an example of every type of anthropological practice.

The first person who agreed to contribute a paper for the symposium was Michael Angrosino himself. He was specifically requested to update the answer to the question he asked two decades ago, "Do applied anthropologists apply anthropology?" His insights are valuable not only because he led the SAS symposium twenty years ago, but also because he has been a very active participant in the growth of applied anthropology since 1975. Over the last twenty years, he has carried out many applied research projects, has recently completed a term as editor of *Human Organization,* and is a member of the Department of Anthropology at the University of South Florida, one of the premier applied anthropology training programs in the United States. I asked him to reflect on what had happened to the authors of the 1975 symposium and to respond again to the question he had posed twenty years ago. The answer he provides is surprising, since he again says, "No!" Read his essay to understand what he perceives to be some of the critical issues for the next twenty years.

WHAT DO APPLIED ANTHROPOLOGISTS APPLY?

In 1975 Angrosino suggested that applied anthropology needs a special body of theory and method that makes it characteristically different from the contributions of other social science disciplines such as economics or psychology (Angrosino 1976:8). Twenty years later he feels the same way. The tendencies toward multifaceted and varied endeavors he noticed in 1975 have continued. He worries in 1995 that sociocultural anthropologists are too eclectic and that the discipline has become indistinguishable from other social sciences. Andrew Miracle, in this volume, suggests in a similar vein that applied anthropologists need to be more concerned about becoming explicitly theoretical, that our use of anthropological techniques has been effective, but at the price of losing our disciplinary center. While I reluctantly agree to some extent with both, I am amazed at the variety of ways in which anthropological principles and techniques are being applied in 1990s. I believe the essays in this volume represent anthropological imagination at its best. They also provide good, clear, practical examples of the nature of applied anthropology.

THE IMPORTANCE OF STUDENTS

Another reason for organizing this symposium arises out of concern for my students who frequently ask the question, "I like anthropology a lot, but what can I do with it?" It seems the discipline has been very successful in turning on students to anthropology, but has been much less successful in helping students prepare for the job market. Between 1948 and 1992, 118,962 B.A.'s and 23,779 M.A.'s were awarded by North American anthropology departments, as compared with only 9,814 Ph.D.'s (Baba 1994:176). The vast majority of our majors will earn B.A.'s. We give them the anthropological perspective, but do we also train them for a nonacademic job market? Should we strive to help students enter the job market? What do we tell aspiring graduate students about the academic job market?

In the end, students are our most important product. We must do well in the classroom, and get the students to spread the word that anthropology's role is important in the modern world. We must help them understand the messages anthropologists offer, but we must also adequately train them for jobs both inside and outside the academy. One area where much improvement needs to be made is in the mentoring process. As David Givens and Timothy Jablonski report in the 1995 Survey of Anthropology Ph.D.'s, "The modal word to describe mentoring was 'nonexistent'" (1995:317). They report that many students complain about the lack of advice they received about the job market especially in academia, but also outside the academy. For an example of this problem, read Christopher Walker's essay in this volume. He insightfully describes the problems of the job market and the head-in-the-sand approach regarding job market advice for aspiring graduate students. Walker suggests that anthropology students no longer can depend on being the Lévi-Straussian "bricoleur" when it comes to finding a suitable job; they need a variety of specific skills for the modern world. At the same time, he has no regrets about getting a Ph.D. in anthropology.

There may not be much mentoring among anthropologists in academic settings, but NAPA has been busy encouraging the development of mentorship relationships between applied anthropology students and practicing anthropologists. There are approximately eighteen Local Practitioner Organizations (LPOs) in the United States with a membership of about 850 persons (Baba 1994:179). LPOs are regional, voluntary organizations of practitioners. Some of the largest, such as the Washington Association of Professional Anthropologists (WAPA), have monthly meetings and publish a newsletter and an annual directory. In the South there are two very active associations, the Mid-South Association of Professional Anthropologists (MSAPA), headquartered in Memphis, and the Sun Coast Organization of Practicing Anthropologists (SCOPA) in the Tampa, Florida region. In 1993, anthropologists in North Carolina, practitioner and academic, established an association (ANCA) that meets twice a year and has an Internet "listserv" for online communication (Wallace 1995). Mentorship programs with LPOs are an invaluable means of establishing a bridge between the academy and practitioner colleagues, as well as helping our students make contacts for the future (Wallace 1995).

Where *are* the non-Ph.D. anthropologists finding jobs? Few anthropology programs keep statistics on what happens to alumni. Recently I asked Internet subscribers of the ANTHRO-L general anthropology discussion list and subscribers of ANTHAP, the SfAA/NAPA discussion list, "Are anthropology students with B.A's and M.A's anthropologists?" Most responses from Ph.D. anthropologists said no, but many people with M.A's and B.A.'s felt they were. Some colleagues remarked that professors have no responsibility toward helping students in the job market beyond teaching them critical thinking.

Why is there hostility to the idea that students without Ph.D's can also practice anthropology? What kind of responsibility do we have in mentoring students for the job market? How much and what kind of training is necessary to make a practicing anthropologist? These are questions currently being debated by many applied anthropologists and must be squarely addressed soon (Baba 1994; Kushner 1994; van Willigen 1991).

Good applied anthropology programs seem to have good internship programs. In the essay by Michael English we see an anthropologist inspired by his experience in a master's program at the University of South Florida. Building on his internship in an urban planning setting in Hillsborough County, Florida, he now has his own urban planning company. Read Bridget Ciaramitaro's essay in this volume for another good example of a person who did not let concerns about what other anthropologists thought get in the way of developing an award-winning, successful consulting business. She got her applied M.A. at the University of Memphis and was clearly well trained for the professional world, despite her initial fears about leaving academia.

Christopher Brown makes a strong case for the importance of bringing together marketing and anthropology skills for the type of work he does in social marketing in Texas. He is passionate about his work and the way he combines these two fields into a successful career. He, too, received his M.A. from the University of South Florida and had an internship experience. The importance of the internship experience for the undergraduate also can be seen from the essay by Susan Emley Keefe, who leads the undergraduate program at Appalachian State University. Internships are an integral part of the applied concentration at ASU and students have participated in them all over the country and in several Latin American countries. Jeff Boyer, also at ASU, explains how the sustainable development program he instituted at ASU has outreach components and how it may have directly helped raise campus awareness in local environmental issues. Boyer has brought together his activist, anthropological concern for the environment and sustainable agriculture and made it accessible for undergraduates. At the same time he adds to the stature and visibility of anthropology on his campus and gives it a multidisciplinary focus.

Another key question, then, is what kind of anthropological training should students be getting? How much theory is necessary? What kind of skills do they need? What kind of training should we give to the overwhelming majority of students who will never get a Ph.D.? Should even the students not seeking an applied focus also receive practical training? The essays in this volume by Mary La Lone, and Melinda Wagner, Shannon Scott, and Danny Wolfe illustrate how undergraduates can employ anthropological concepts and methods in practical settings with surprisingly far-reaching effects. Their success is wonderful not only for them but also for the discipline of anthropology as well. These essays also show the innovative kind of course work that can be done to carry anthropology beyond the classroom to the community.

The successful strategy for getting archeology into the public sector is mirrored in the success described at ASU. Modern, "applied" archeology fits well into the type of agenda Angrosino argues for sociocultural applied anthropology. Archeology has been quite successful in developing a specific practicing niche outside academia, based on a demand for specific skills to protect the nation's archeological heritage. Gyrisco (1989) states that the federal government alone employs 300–400 archeologists.

There are today many job opportunities for anthropologists outside of academia. Marietta Baba (1994:177–78), in an essay on the structure of practitioner anthropology, used several strategies for estimating the number of Ph.D. practitioner anthropologists in nonacademic settings. She concluded that 30 percent of the total number of Ph.D. anthropologists were practitioner anthropologists, about 2,100 of them in 1992, and that there would be a total of 3,000 by the year 2000. Table 1 depicts how the Ph.D. practitioner anthropologists were employed in 1992.

From Table 1, we can see that the public health/health services field is one of the largest for practicing anthropologists. The concern for the medical field is reflected in this volume with essays by Sharon Glick Miller, Mary Anglin, Robert Morrow, and Richard Persico and Roger Branch. The essay by Sharon Miller examines the changing nature of clinical anthropology and the need for training that takes into account the special roles of applied, clinical anthropologists. Like others in the symposium, she argues that there be a more explicit integration of theory into classroom discussion, and she decries the dearth of texts in the field. Integrating texts are needed, she says, so that the subdiscipline of clinically applied anthropology can move forward.

In the essay by Mary Anglin, we see the traditional role of ethnographer being played out in a health setting. Moreover, we also see how applied anthropology not only generates data for theoretical or applied outcomes, but also how the ethnographer must struggle to maintain an ethical balance between the research demands of the clients and the reality of the subjects of those studied. In the end, the applied anthropolo-

Table 1

Substantive Job Focus Areas for Practicing Anthropologists, 1992

Job Focus Areas	Percentage of Practicing Anthropologists
Evaluation	31
Public Health/Health Services	29
Social Impact Assessment	24
Private Sector	23
Agricultural Development	14
Natural Resources	13
Education	12

Note: More than one response could be given.
Source: Baba 1994:178

gist remains an anthropologist cognizant of and dedicated to the reality of the subject's problems—just like all anthropologists.

The essay by Richard Persico and Roger Branch reveals an anthropologist and a sociologist collaborating on a course for professional medical service providers that shows how the anthropological perspective can still gather converts. Nevertheless, one does not have to be a convert to practice sound, ethically responsible fieldwork, as illustrated in Christopher Toumey's essay, "Praying with Creationists." His work brings home the importance of doing fieldwork in our backyard. Hans Baer invokes the well-known Laura Nader article (1972) about "studying up the system" to emphasize the importance of the "partisan observation" he is doing among the faculty at the University of Arkansas, Little Rock, where he is a professor.

Relevance was an important catch word in academia twenty years ago. It is no less important in the 1990s, but its referent has changed somewhat. The research product must also have relevance to the people who fund the research and pay the salaries and fees to the researchers. There is a more urgent demand for anthropologists to make their research relevant. Students want to know what they can do with anthropology when they graduate, besides shooting for an academic position.

Administrators want to know why anthropology should be considered as important as engineering or history. Trustees insist on a correlation between numbers of majors and numbers of faculty positions. Broadening our audience (clientele) beyond other anthropologists and their students is important. Survival requires it. The audience includes people in business, school teachers, other academics, university administrators, local and federal governments, but perhaps most of all everyday citizens—including taxpayers. One thing that applied anthropology does best is show local people the value and power of anthropology.

APPLIED ANTHROPOLOGY: A GROWTH INDUSTRY

Applied anthropology is called the "fifth subdiscipline" because of its practice orientation and because anthropological practice crosscuts the entire discipline anthropology. Physical anthropologists are found in health settings or forensic settings, for example. Archeologists are heavily involved in the cultural resource management in the public sector. Linguistic anthropologists can be found working in educational settings, to mention only a few. The skills of practicing sociocultural anthropologists are more general and there are many models by which they are entering the nonacademic job market. They can be found in a wide range of settings.

Anthropology departments are probably in a good position to maintain or increase the number of faculty and students over the next two decades, but anthropology departments will have to be seen as relevant to contemporary issues. According to the 1994 survey of chairpersons of anthropology departments, over the next twenty-five years, sociocultural anthropology will "be retained only if its practitioners also work in more applied areas; . . . [furthermore, departments will find it advantageous to] involve [their] faculty—and/or take the lead—in university-wide programs, such as sustainable development, world ecology, environmental studies, etc." (Givens and Mahaney 1994:294).

Honggang Yang in this volume discusses his work at the Carter Presidential Center in Atlanta on international peace issues. In the process he developed important skills in dispute processing and now is a coordinator of the Conflict Resolution Program at the MacGregor School of Antioch University. Conflict resolution is now a major growth area

Well, *Do* They?
The New Applied Anthropology
Twenty Years Later

Michael V. Angrosino

The most important development in the twenty years of the new applied anthropology has been the emergence of practitioners who are engaged in applications of anthropology on a full-time basis outside the university. This trend has led to the proliferation of training programs in applied anthropology that prepare students for nonacademic careers. The history of these two trends has been documented and analyzed by Baba (1994), Bennett (1988), Hyland and Kirkpatrick (1989), Kushner (1994), Leacock, Gonzalez, and Kushner (1974), van Willigen (1988), and Wolfe (1978). As background to this year's discussion of practicing anthropology in the South, it may be instructive to review the way the participants in the 1975 SAS symposium "Do Applied Anthropologists Apply Anthropology?" (Angrosino 1976) foresaw these developments.

John Bushnell (1976:16), for example, predicted "a need for anthropological paraprofessionals and technicians functioning in a capacity analogous to that of the physician's assistant, laboratory technician, or occupational therapist." Robert Wulff (1976:47) offered a somewhat more exalted list of roles: "an elected planning commissioner, a civil servant position in a municipal planning department, or an appointment to a citizens' advisory board." Edward Spicer (1976:133) also advocated anthropologists moving into "policy-making or policy-advising roles." But they were all simply suggesting position titles; none of them said what such anthropologists would do in those positions. This skirting of an issue that would loom so large in the evolution of the discipline is no doubt due to the fact that the symposium participants were almost all academics who took it for granted that academics would retain control over the domain of application. Indeed, although they spoke of the "practice" of anthropology, they referred to those who did so not as "practitioners" but as the "non-academically employed," as if to emphasize that the universe of applied anthropology was to be defined in relation to academe.

Of the panelists, only E. B. Eiselein, a media consultant, was at the time "non-academically employed," although he illustrated his main points with a project that he had conducted while still affiliated with a university. Both Spicer and John van Willigen had been employed outside of academe earlier in their careers, but they wrote in 1975 as academics. Wulff moved on to a successful career as a practitioner, but in 1975 he held an academic position. He has, moreover, remained the practitioner with perhaps the most active links to university-based applied anthropologists.

Several models for training the new applied anthropologist were advanced in 1975, all of them sharing the assumption that applied anthropologists would remain researchers. That there might arise a class of practitioner whose primary roles would be as *consumers* rather than as *producers* of research did not figure into their calculations.

Bushnell (1976:15), for example, discussed in some detail the establishment of "professional schools of anthropology bearing a resemblance . . . to existing schools of . . . social work, nursing, medicine, law, or engineering." Lucy Cohen (1976:31) emphasized the need for research collaboration between universities and public health/human service agencies, and the expansion of continuing education programs in anthropology among members of other professions. John van Willigen (1976:90) advocated a type of anthropological course work that would "simulate the realities of the applied situation." Hazel Weidman (1976:116) preferred to locate training programs in existing professional schools. Spicer advocated training in policy-program analysis and policy-program design, but saw such training as a sequence of courses in a conventional graduate program in anthropology, not as an autonomous training program.

The participants assumed that applications would take place in the public sector, a logical position in that era of expanding government presence in the health and human services. Even Eiselein, when speaking of the media, referred almost exclusively to public broadcasting. None of the lists of model professional schools included business schools, although work in the private sector has come to be a steadily growing minority occupation among members of the Society for Applied Anthropology (Harding 1994).

The participants took it for granted that training would be at the Ph.D. level, which was the appropriate level for the academically based anthropologist. But such training has instead flourished in M.A. programs, creating a large cadre of M.A.-level "technicians," with implications of a professional caste hierarchy that have not been fully explored in the literature. The prospects for and desirability of applied training at the B.A. level have also not been sufficiently examined.

In organizing the 1975 symposium, I made a conscious effort to achieve "four field" representation. As it turned out, the linguistic anthropologist (Dorothy Clement) did not stray too far from the principles set forth by other sociocultural anthropologists. But the physical anthropologist (Louise Robbins) and the archeologist (Hester Davis) made it clear that their branches of the discipline were special cases.

Robbins (1976:20) asserted that the very concept of applied anthropology is "an epiphenomenon of sociocultural anthropology," not because physical anthropologists did not engage in application, but because they viewed such application as a natural aspect of "the diversity that constitutes physical anthropology." Physical anthropologists had long taught in medical or dental schools where their teaching and research placed them at the service of professional or institutional interests extrinsic to anthropology. Those physical anthropologists who worked in genetic counseling, forensics, or human engineering considered themselves to be scholarly researchers rather than "practitioners," since research in these fields had always been viewed as an intrinsic part of physical anthropology, not as a new application.

Although advances in genetics and primate ethology have, if anything, enhanced the "marketability" of biological anthropologists, most of them would probably reaffirm Robbins's point of view; they do not see themselves as "practitioners" insofar as they continue to work largely in the context of the university classroom or the research laboratory. They do not publish in *Human Organization* and are typically not involved in applied training programs, even when they are, as individuals, members of departments of anthropology.

Davis wrote just as the impact of the national Environmental Protection Act was being felt, and she heralded the emergence of "public" archeology. She asserted that the need for archeologists to preserve the record of the past was not "a responsibility for the sake of the discipline" (1976:73) but rather a new, flexible, growing *profession*. The shift from "discipline" to "profession" was thus much more clearly articulated by the archeologist than by any of the sociocultural anthropologists on the panel. Indeed, the proliferation of positions for archeologists in both government and private consultation has made for a highly visible, organized, and influential archeological practice wing. Practicing archeologists are, like the physical anthropologists, convinced that they are applying the discipline in which they were trained. Archeologists hired by the Park Service, for example, are *doing archeology*. Cultural anthropologists, by contrast, are rarely hired under that title, and the things they have been trained to do are things that people from any number of social science disciplines have also been trained to do. Weidman noted in passing that she preferred to call herself an "applied social scientist" rather than an "applied anthropologist." She took pride in the breadth of her training and professional competencies, but practicing anthropologists nowadays often lament that the greater the breadth of their training and experiences, the weaker the ties that bind them to anthropology.

Can practitioners maintain an identification with the discipline? They should, in the ideal at least, keep current with the theories, methods, and substantive data of anthropology. But our methods are now common property; "ethnography" has been shared so promiscuously that its parentage is now essentially a moot point. Moreover, most of us apply ourselves in areas in which sociology, psychology, economics, or political science have the more relevant bodies of substantive knowledge.

Which leaves, alas, theory—the very thing applied anthropologists were never supposed to be any good at. The problem is not, however, that applied anthropologists are poor theoreticians; it is, rather, that anthropological theory is no longer entirely suitable for the purposes of applied anthropology. Practicing anthropologists sometimes make a game attempt to assert the "anthropological difference"—some aspect of a particular project that could only have been the result of the input of one steeped in anthropology. But the "anthropological difference" more often than not boils down to a few truisms about "holism" or "getting the insiders' perspective," neither of which is specific to anthropology at this point in our history, and neither of which is used in any but the most commonsensical way.

Over the past twenty years we have seen a gradual movement of applied anthropology away from the theoretical mainstream of the discipline. Theory is consequently threatened with becoming ever more esoteric since it is no longer in dialogue with those in a position to test some of its hypotheses in "real world" situations. At the same time, practitioners are in danger of committing the fallacy of assuming that generic common sense will always be more useful than "ivory tower concepts." In the old days, functionalist theory, or acculturation theory, or the various species of social and cultural evolutionary theory were, whatever their limitations, well suited for application in the directed culture change projects that engaged applied anthropologists. But the 1970s, the era of the ascendancy of the new applied anthropology in areas of domestic policy and the institutionalized expansion of service bureaucracies, was also the period in anthropological theory dominated by French structuralism. I know of no applied anthropologists rash enough to have tried to introduce Lévi-Strauss to the world of program evaluation and needs assessment. In our own day, there has been at least a token effort to harmonize postmodern theory with applied anthropology (Johannsen 1992); but such a sporting effort has not touched off a trend. It has, indeed, sparked a strong criticism (Singer 1994) that will probably help to chill any further rapprochement between the postmodernists and the practitioners.

I suggest that the intellectual coherence of sociocultural anthropology, which was more or less taken for granted in 1975, no longer obtains, and that as the discipline itself fragments and its pieces merge with the concerns of other disciplines, it becomes less and less meaningful to speak of an applied *anthropology*. In 1975, it was assumed that the new applied anthropologist had to be proficient in both anthropology and a related professional field of application (e.g., public health, education, urban planning). Might it now be the case that the practitioner must be conversant with a cafeteria of methods, theories, and bodies of substantive data that transcend any one "home" discipline—that *include* but cannot be limited to materials traditionally associated with anthropology? If so, it is likely that practitioners put together that package of methodological and analytical skills that best suit them in their particular applications and that each such package will be discernibly different from all others.

This embrace of eclecticism was clearly envisioned by the 1975 panelists, although Wulff (1976:48) wisely warned that "eclecticism entails both benefits and costs." The most important cost was seen as a kind of information overload, a problem that has only grown more burdensome as new technologies unforeseen in 1975 provide us with instantaneous access to a seemingly unlimited pool of information. Wulff has often spoken in later conference presentations of his preference for generically labeling the ideal practitioner as a "creative problem solver," rather than as one conversant with the whole of any single academic discipline. Some bits of anthropological knowledge would be included in the bag of tricks of this creative problem solver, but such a person would clearly not be an applied *anthropologist* in the same sense that a Sol Tax or a Margaret Mead could be so designated.

The 1975 panelists' assumption that applied anthropology would maintain its academic base is now outmoded. The Society for Applied Anthropology remains a preserve of academics, as might be expected for a traditionally structured "learned society"; but even so, nearly one-third of the SfAA membership is not university-based, a proportion that has grown steadily over the past decade and shows every indication of continuing to increase (Harding 1994). Practitioners tend to join Local Practitioner Organizations, which provide peer group support rather than traditional "scholarly exchange." And sociocultural practitioners have engaged in an adaptive radiation, filling dozens of professional niches, the diversity of which would seem to preclude their coming together at a single meeting or conference. We are left with a situation in which the driving force is a job market in which people need a range of skills that are not necessarily the property of any one discipline. Once employed, they will eventually receive more specialized (and probably technical rather than academic) training. But as they get such training, they move away from the "home" discipline to an extent that might have been unthinkable in 1975. Graduate training in applied anthropology may simply indicate that recipients are good at being "trained," since they have spent several extra years in learning how to learn. This is not an entirely bad place to be—it certainly gives us lots of options—but it is a far cry from where our ideals of 1975 suggested we should be.

So, do applied anthropologists apply anthropology? My answer as of 1995 is "no," if by anthropology we mean what passes for a coherent body of theory, method, and substantive data taught under that disciplinary rubric. It seems to me that the greatest glory of the anthropological perspective has always been its inclusiveness. But that is also the seed of its failure as a source of professional practice: we now often find ourselves indistinguishable from our colleagues. The eclecticism that was thrust on applied anthropologists twenty years ago has now caught up with the rest of the discipline.

What are we to do? I offer the following suggestions as a starting point for discussion, not as a finished agenda.

1. Focus practice on the things we have historically done best. Reclaim the concept of culture. Make ourselves central to the discourse on multiculturalism that is at the heart of planning and service delivery in virtually all fields of contemporary social policy.

2. Concentrate on issues in the health and human services to which the anthropological perspective is most clearly attuned: those that deal with questions of race and ethnicity, gender, cross-cultural communication.

3. Let go of the four-field approach. Recognize that sociocultural applied anthropologists can continue to honor their historical kinship with physical anthropologists and archeologists, even as they admit that the lore of those fields is not necessarily more central to their application than is that of any other discipline.

4. Focus on working cooperatively with people in communities or other "natural" groups, which means working primarily with and for the "powerless." Some of our number may well rise to positions of power, but let's be honest—the instincts and inclinations that lead most of us to choose anthropology as a field of study in the first place are the same instincts and inclinations that preadapt us to play roles of advocacy, support, advisement. We are, in C. Wright Mills's (1959) memorable phrase, better suited to be "advisors to the king" rather than "philosopher kings."

5. Anthropologists have always been called on not only to understand but also to communicate with "the other." Why can't we play that same role in our own society—as translators of the opaque jargon that sepa-

rates our academic colleagues from those they would influence? In effect, let's use the fact that we have perforce mastered the technobabble of a dozen different academic fields, and assume the role of "knowledge transfer specialist" (Hobbs 1980). We don't necessarily need *new* knowledge—we need to make sense of what we've already got. Perhaps the perfect "applied" graduate dissertation or thesis should not be a piece of "original" research at all, but a brief and lucid presentation of some current scientific imbroglio suitable for an audience of, for example, lay civic activists or politicians. In the old days, if you wanted to know about the religion, the arts, the politics, the economics, or the kinship patterns of the proverbial "exotic tribe," you certainly didn't go on your own to interview the shaman, the craftsman, the headman, the farmer, or the clan elder—you asked the anthropologist, who put it all together and gave you a sense of what it felt like to be an insider in that community. Couldn't we do the analogous thing now by becoming servers to the general public in the cafeteria line of modern social science?

REFERENCES

Angrosino, Michael V. 1976. The Evolution of the New Applied Anthropology. In *Do Applied Anthropologists Apply Anthropology?,* ed. Michael V. Angrosino, pp. 1–9. Athens: University of Georgia Press.

Baba, Marietta. 1994. The Fifth Subdiscipline: Anthropological Practice and the Future of Anthropology. *Human Organization* 53:174–85.

Bennett, Linda. 1988. *Bridges for Changing Times: Local Practitioner Organizations in American Anthropology.* Washington, DC: American Anthropological Association.

Bushnell, John. 1976. The Art of Practicing Anthropology. In *Do Applied Anthropologists Apply Anthropology?,* pp. 10–16.

Clement, Dorothy C. 1976. Cognitive Anthropology and Applied Problems in Education. In *Do Applied Anthropologists Apply Anthropology?,* pp. 53–71.

Cohen, Lucy M. 1976. Conflict and Planned Change in the Development of Community Health Services. In *Do Applied Anthropologists Apply Anthropology?,* pp. 22–33.

Davis, Hester A. 1976. Applied Archaeology: New Approaches, New Directions, New Needs. In *Do Applied Anthropologists Apply Anthropology?,* pp. 72–80.

Eiselein, E. B. 1976. Broadcasting and Applied Media Anthropology. In *Do Applied Anthropologists Apply Anthropology?,* pp. 92–104.

Harding, Joe. 1994. *SfAA Membership Survey.* Oklahoma City: Society for Applied Anthropology.

Hobbs, Nicholas. 1980. *Knowledge Transfer and the Policy Process.* Nashville, TN: Vanderbilt Institute for Public Policy Studies.

Hyland, Stanley, and Sean Kirkpatrick, eds. 1989. *Guide to Training Programs in the Applications of Anthropology,* 3d ed. Oklahoma City: Society for Applied Anthropology.

Johannsen, Agneta. 1992. Applied Anthropology and Post-Modernist Ethnography. *Human Organization* 51:71–81.

Kushner, Gilbert. 1994. Training Programs for the Practice of Anthropology. *Human Organization* 53:186–91.

Leacock, Eleanor, Nancie L. Gonzalez, and Gilbert Kushner, eds. 1974. *Training Programs for New Opportunities in Applied Anthropology.* Washington, DC: American Anthropological Association and Society for Applied Anthropology.

Mills, C. Wright. 1959. *The Sociological Imagination.* New York: Grove Press.

Robbins, Louise M. 1976. The Nature of "Applied" Physical Anthropology. In *Do Applied Anthropologists Apply Anthropology?,* pp. 17–22.

Singer, Merrill. 1994. Community-Centered Praxis: Toward an Alternative Non-Dominative Applied Anthropology. *Human Organization* 53:336–44.

Spicer, Edward H. 1976. Anthropology and the Policy Process. In *Do Applied Anthropologists Apply Anthropology?,* pp. 118–33.

van Willigen, John. 1976. Applied Anthropology and Community Development Administration: A Critical Assessment. In *Do Applied Anthropologists Apply Anthropology?,* pp. 81–91.

———. 1988. Types of Programs. In *Anthropology for Tomorrow,* ed. Robert Trotter, pp. 8–19. Washington, DC: American Anthropological Association.

Weidman, Hazel H. 1976. In Praise of the Double Bind Inherent in Anthropological Application. In *Do Applied Anthropologists Apply Anthropology?,* pp. 105–17.

Wolfe, Alvin W. 1978. The Jobs of Applied Anthropologists. *Practicing Anthropology* 1:14–16.

Wulff, Robert M. 1976. Anthropology in the Urban Planning Process: A Review and an Agenda. In *Do Applied Anthropologists Apply Anthropology?,* pp. 34–52.

A Southern View of Organizations and Change: Testifying to Theory

Andrew W. Miracle

Utilizing a single case study, my goal is to demonstrate connections among training, practice, and theory in applied anthropology in the South. To do so, I shall describe my personal academic experience because mine was not atypical for anthropology graduate students at the University of Florida in the 1970s. Moreover, I suspect that it was not too different from experiences at many other institutions at that time.

THE STUDENTS

Many of the students, especially those who would eventually develop career interests in applied anthropology, had come to the department from recent experiences in the Peace Corps or from work experiences in social services. For example, I had worked in Bolivia in a rural development program sponsored by the Methodist Church. I later learned that many of the faculty, especially those with an applied orientation, also shared early career experience in social service professions and several had ties to overseas church work.

In addition to overseas experiences and involvement with social issues or social services, it seems on reflection that most of the anthropology graduate students at the University of Florida in those days were southerners. Our widely shared experiences and perspectives helped to create a student culture that was decidedly southern, socially liberal, and pragmatic in terms of problem solving. On the basis solely of my own experience, I believe that the students at that time were more cooperative than those of more recent generations. Study groups and information sharing were the norm, and individual competition was minimal. There was great emphasis on sociability, and the relationships among students might best be described as conforming to the model of the southern extended family.

Perhaps what I am describing as a student culture influenced by its southern roots resulted because the department in Gainesville was primarily regional in its stature and appeal in those days. The Columbia "brain drain" had only recently brought Solon T. Kimball, Elizabeth M. Eddy, and Charles Wagley to campus. The faculty was still small in number and several years passed before it began to achieve national recognition.

THE FACULTY

Until the late 1970s, the anthropology faculty at the University of Florida probably never numbered more than a dozen or so. I cannot describe the applied orientation of the entire faculty here, but I do want to mention a few of the many who contributed to my applied education. All of these individuals are now deceased or retired; however, all had been involved in projects of directed change at some point in their careers, as had several others in the department (e.g., Paul Doughty and Otto Von Mering).

Bill Carter valued applied anthropology, though most of his early career had been spent doing ethnographic fieldwork or serving as an administrator. In the early 1970s, however, he embarked on a series of research projects dealing with the effects of coca-chewing and the use of cannabis. Some of his students continue to work on related topics today.

I remember sitting in his office one day when he talked at length about the benefits that resulted from anthropologists moving from academic to nonacademic settings and back again. He remarked, and it was true at the time, that many anthropologists expected to make such shifts during their careers. What he did not foresee in 1971 was the impending change in academic employment that would render such moves virtually impossible.

Carter privately described his theoretical orientation as eclectic, while I would describe his work as descriptive and particularistic. Moreover, his work reflected the general ethnographic orientation of the department at that time.

Sol Kimball took a rational approach to teaching anthropological skills. He used examples, often from his own research experiences, as particularistic models. Overall, Kimball's orientation was descriptive but suggestive of generalization. Kimball (1960) thought that Darwin's inductive approach was the preferable research strategy for anthropologists, working from particular data to general principles. It is, however, difficult even today for me to specify the principles that guided his work.

Kimball taught us a great deal about how to do fieldwork, often referencing his own applied experiences. (For examples, see Arensberg and Kimball 1965.) Kimball also taught us a great deal about individual interactions and small group behavior.

Kimball viewed all social behavior as sets of reciprocal systems. He taught us that reciprocal systems were affected both by formal status relations and by innate (i.e., biologically based) human differences. He frequently talked about biological rhythms and said that leadership involved the ability to regulate the interaction rates of others. Much of his understanding of such behavior was grounded in the work of Eliot Chapple (Chapple 1970; Chapple and Coon 1942).

There is little doubt, however, that Kimball's greatest contribution was to instill a critical awareness and appreciation of ritual and its power. We read about and discussed ritual events, and we were required to study, describe, and analyze ritual in our own lives.

Chuck Wagley was the consummate fieldworker and ethnographer. While he is not often remembered as an applied anthropologist, much of his ethnography dealt with modernization and culture change. After moving to Florida, he also became active in applied research, serving as co-principal investigator with Kimball on the NIE-funded School and Community Project (Kimball and Wagley 1974). I was one of several student fieldworkers on that project.

From Wagley I internalized an etiquette for comportment in the field, as well as a set of ethical considerations for dealing with a variety of professional situations. In interactions with colleagues, graduate students, and individuals in the community under investigation, Wagley's first concern always seemed to be the ethical consideration of others.

It gradually became apparent to me that such behavior inevitably had beneficial effects on research outcomes. Treated with respect, kindness, and generosity, others generally become more accessible and supportive of the researcher's own goals and objectives—even though they may never understand why the silly anthropologist has such concerns. To this day, when I am facing a decision with unclear professional demands, I ask myself what Dr. Wagley would have done.

The NIE project was designed to study the effects of court-ordered school desegregation; working with Kimball and Wagley and a large team of fieldworkers on that project changed the direction of my career.

Liz Eddy became a significant role model in my graduate education when I had the opportunity to work for a year on a project on which she was co-principal investigator. I was one of several fieldworkers studying educational innovation and the diffusion of innovations at a number of school sites. In this capacity I followed her into organizations, watched her, and assisted her as an aide. My role was not unlike that of a drummer in a traditional sucking cure assisting the master shaman.

It was through observing her at work and through the feedback I received on my own early efforts that I began to understand the use of models in practice. For example, I had read Eddy's work (1969) on ritual in the professionalization of teachers, but as I worked with her I saw it for myself. She was there to reinforce my observations or subtly indicate finer points that I might have missed initially on my own. There is no doubt that this protracted one-on-one mentoring was a significant factor in the development of my skills and perspectives as an applied anthropologist.

THE CURRICULUM

It might be inferred that most of the significant lessons about applied anthropology at the University of Florida in the 1970s resulted from informal encounters with students and individual relationships with faculty, especially since if one examines the curriculum, there was, in fact, no formal course work on applied subjects.

The official curriculum was designed to be holistic. Graduate students were required to take courses in the four-field approach and were held responsible for general information from all four at the time of M.A.-level examinations. Since these exams were the gateway to doctoral study, it was imperative that a student pass all four parts of the examination. There was no exam for applied anthropology.

It was assumed by most members of the department that there were applications to be made from each of the subdisciplines' base of knowledge. (For example, see Angrosino 1976.) Perhaps this point of view explains why there was no perceived need to design a specialized applied curriculum.

If you were interested in an applied career, you chose an advisor and selected courses that would enhance your applied knowledge and the potential for future employment. The courses you might select focused on the interests of individual faculty, such as culture and community, organizations, culture change, or an institutional focus such as educational or medical anthropology.

I want to elaborate on what I learned to be the primary concerns of applied anthropology: the nature of organizations and the nature of change. I recognize that applied anthropology for some involves other focuses. In this essay, however, I shall limit my discussion to these principles for two reasons. First, this is what was stressed at the University of Florida in the 1970s while I was in graduate school. Second, my own applied work has been limited to working with organizations in efforts to direct change processes.

THE VIEW OF ORGANIZATIONS

At the University of Florida there seemed to be a widely shared view of organizations that one might absorb in any number of courses or from any of several faculty members. As I reflect on it now, that view was that most formal organizations are similar in significant ways and that they might be understood through the application of one of a few models. Consider the following examples as indicative.

The extended family model was a functionalist understanding of organizations. This model was a favorite of many southern students and of those faculty members who had done extensive work in the South. According to this model, one could best view organizations as a set of reciprocal systems. Moreover, organizations ought to exhibit specialized statuses and roles with delegation from a centralized authority, which was not necessarily paternalistic. Adherence to shared values and common goals should promote the enlightened self-interest of individuals in the organization's substructures.

Another functionalist model compared the organization to the rural, small town. This model stressed the basic variations in cultural traditions that might affect the structure of organizations as well as their organizational culture. Just as basic town patterns (e.g., New England village, southern courthouse square, and Midwestern crossroads town) reflected the cultural differences of their founders (Arensberg 1955), so too might organizations.

Finally, there was what might be called the northern urban dysfunctional model of organizations. According to this model, some organizations lacked the centralized focus and centripetal forces to function effectively, perhaps because they were too large to remain cohesive. In other cases, there might be a lack of sufficient common ritual to regulate interactions, promote commitment to shared values, and to focus individual energies on common goals. The organization could also be exhibiting *anomie,* the result of recent chaotic change.

Certainly the description of these models sounds more than a little parochial, and perhaps a bit naive. The assumption, however, was that there were relatively few variations on the general theme of structure and function of organizations. Therefore, one of these models was likely to fit almost any situation one might encounter. Armed with these few models, students might enter any organization with the confidence that one's understanding should quickly become clarified.

THE VIEW OF CHANGE

While as graduate students we were exposed to cultural materialism and cultural ecology, the dominant though often unstated theoretical position of most faculty members was structural-functionalism. This was certainly the case of the applied anthropologists. In course work and the mentoring that resulted from working on applied research projects, students were likely to formulate a single understanding of change. That is, reading about Vicos and observing innovation in schools provided the same models for understanding change.

What effects change and what is changeable? We learned that change can result from external or internal factors. Moreover, the functionalist model led us to assume that a change in the environment or in any single area of an organization might have consequences for the rest of the system. Of course, working from this model it was difficult to predict change with any specificity.

Understanding the reciprocal systems of an organization, however, gave us insight into the potential for change. Though it was unstated by the applied faculty, it was clear that the key to understanding reciprocal systems was materialistic. Who controls resources and what are the nature of those resources? That is, who is dependent on whom for what?

It is significant that in discussions of change there was always a consideration of ethics, implicitly if not explicitly. What kinds of change can and should be promoted? Who will be affected by proposed change and in what ways? While it is true that these considerations may have been based on rather naive understandings of ethical principles, at least they occurred. Moreover, it is not clear to me that the profession in general has made much progress in this area since the 1970s.

SHAMANIC AND ACADEMIC WAYS OF KNOWING AND INITIATING CHANGE

In other publications (Miracle 1982, in press) I have compared the training and work of applied anthropologists to that of shamans. While I proposed such comparisons with serious intent, I sometimes fear that the slightly tongue-in-cheek approach of these articles may have dissuaded serious consideration by some. Therefore, I want to restate my belief, with total sincerity, that applied anthropologists are to directed change in organizations as shamans are to directed change in the statuses of individuals, families, and traditional communities.

There are, however, some significant differences in shamanic and academic ways of knowing and curing. Shamans acquire knowledge through an individualized vision which is usually analyzed and supplemented through an apprenticeship with a mentor. On the other hand, the academic model of knowing relies heavily on internalizing an existing theoretical perspective (i.e., that of one's advisor) and memorizing previously accumulated data assumed to be accurate. This is a conservative system that tends to replicate each generation of scholars with only minor changes sufficient to allow the young to pretend that they are different from their elders. It also allows the younger generation to distinguish itself enough to create a demand for its services. Any major advances tend to occur as a result of data accumulation, especially that tied to new technological developments.

My learning experiences at the University of Florida contained both academic and shamanic elements. I acquired the "big picture" with Kimball and Wagley in a fairly typical academic fashion. I believe I benefitted greatly from my apprenticeships with them and with Liz Eddy. Also, I believe I learned a great deal from my peers, not only in studying together but also while working as colleagues on research teams.

TRANSLATING PERSONAL EFFECTIVENESS INTO NOMOTHETIC PRINCIPLES

My education at the University of Florida more than twenty years ago has served me well as an applied anthropologist. During the past fifteen years I have been able to work successfully with dozens of organizations—large and small, for-profit and not-for-profit. I give much credit for any effectiveness on my part to the opportunity to work as a shaman's apprentice with a number of effective anthropologists willing to serve as mentors.

Much of my work with organizations now seems to be intuitive—what to look for, what questions to ask, how to comport myself, which symbols to exhibit. I suggest, however, that such skills were learned and are not, as others might imply, innate. That is, I believe applied anthropology to be primarily a science, not an art.

The shamanic type of apprenticeship might produce such skills, but what about the academic aspects of my graduate training? Where are they demonstrated today? More to the point, are there any lessons from my experience that might be used in designing applied anthropology programs? What is the relation between effectiveness and the generalization of nomothetic principles?

From the foregoing account it might seem that there was a dearth of overt theory promulgated in the training of applied anthropology students at the University of Florida in the 1970s. In fact, except in the required course on anthropological theories, the word was seldom spoken in classes or in conversations with faculty.

As students we were given models of organizations and models of change that could be applied to most situations, as well as models for understanding certain types of behavior. The use of models, however, does not constitute theory any more than does the shaman's use of visions and symbolic paraphernalia. Models are derived from theory as portrayals of possible relationships.

Today I consciously apply analytic models in my work with organizations, and for the most part I continue to use the models I learned in the 1970s. Moreover, I have come to realize that those models are grounded in a set of assumptions that stem directly from the holistic elements of my graduate school training, even though I did not consciously integrate those elements for many years.

In my case it seems that theory arose from practice, or was at least refined and reinforced by the continuous testing of hypotheses during practice. A similar experience would be the case of an experienced shaman developing a psychosocial theory of healing while testing various hypotheses on clients.

A difference between us and shamans, however, is that we are expected to formalize our theories, share them with colleagues and students, and engage in the scientific process of testing and rejecting those hypotheses. Moreover, doing so is essential if applied anthropology is to continue to grow and gain acceptance both inside and outside academia. Yet as a student of applied anthropology who continues to read the professional journals and related publications, it seems to me that the profession continues to be dominated by typologies and models, and that there have been relatively few attempts to articulate what might be called applied theory. (For examples and discussion, see Eddy and Partridge 1987; van Willigen 1986.)

Why is there a dearth of theory in applied anthropology? If my graduate training in the 1970s was typical, it is no wonder we lack theory today. I seldom heard specific expressions of theory. What I encountered was Boasian particularism or veiled structural-functionalism with an occasional hint of materialistic notions. There were no systematic theoretical statements leading to hypothesis testing. Such was not considered necessary, or even desirable, twenty-five years ago.

It now seems to me that it is time for applied anthropologists to become more explicitly theoretical. I say explicitly since hidden theory, such as I encountered in the 1970s, is no more helpful than an absence of theory in advancing science. Only explicitly stated theory can provide testable hypotheses. Moreover, if everyone has to tease out an individual theoretical position, it makes the advance of knowledge more difficult.

I have described the culture at the University of Florida in the 1970s: functionalist like southern families, descriptive and particularistic like southern folk-tales, with a southern emphasis on personalism and public etiquette. The pedagogical experience was firmly rooted in time and place.

My conclusion is that how we teach and what we teach are interactive elements of programmatic content with long-lasting implications for individual students—including their theoretical orientation. Thus we need to attend to the latent levels of education as well as to the public manifestations of a program's purpose and formal curriculum.

Such is my testimony. I plan to continue to practice applied anthropology in organizations. And, I hope that I shall continue to learn from this practice. Amen.

REFERENCES

Angrosino, Michael V., ed. 1976. *Do Applied Anthropologists Apply Anthropology?* Athens: University of Georgia Press.

Arensberg, Conrad M. 1955. American Communities. *American Anthropologist* 57:6:1143–60.

Arensberg, Conrad M., and Solon T. Kimball. 1965. *Culture and Community.* New York: Harcourt, Brace, Jovanovich.

Chapple, Eliot D. 1970. *Culture and Biological Man.* New York: Holt, Rinehart & Winston.

Chapple, Eliot D., and Carleton S. Coon. 1942. *Principles of Anthropology.* New York: Henry Holt & Co.

Eddy, Elizabeth M. 1969. *Becoming a Teacher.* New York: Teachers College Press.

Eddy, Elizabeth M., and William L. Partridge, eds. 1987. *Applied Anthropology in America,* 2d ed. New York: Columbia University Press.

Kimball, Solon T. 1960. Darwin and the Future of Education. *Educational Forum* Nov:59–72.

Kimball, Solon T., and Charles Wagley, eds. 1974. *Race and Culture in School and Community.* Washington, DC: Office of Education, U.S. Department of Health, Education and Welfare.

Miracle, Andrew W. 1982. The Making of Shamans and Applied Anthropologists. *Practicing Anthropology* 5:1:18–19.

————. in press. Applied Anthropologist: A Shaman to Organizations. In *Research Frontiers in Anthropology,* ed. Carol R. Ember, Melvin Ember, and Peter N. Peregrine. Englewood Cliffs, NJ: Prentice Hall.

van Willigen, John. 1986. *Applied Anthropology: An Introduction.* South Hadley, MA: Bergin and Garvey.

Activist Praxis and Anthropological Knowledge

Mary K. Anglin

This essay argues a simple point: applied settings offer more than the opportunity to engage anthropological knowledge in the context of practice, as important as that endeavor has proven to be. Practicing anthropologists *extend and develop theory* by applying anthropological concepts across the grain of practical experience and by allowing such settings to reflect back their own nuanced versions of social and cultural life. (See Bourdieu 1972 for an elegant articulation of this point.)

For example, in a recent issue of *Medical Anthropological Quarterly* edited by Evelyn Barbee, the authors examined contemporary contexts of health care in the United States—home-based care and nursing as work and research setting, in these instances—as potent sites for the analysis of race and racism (Barbee 1993a, 1993b; Clark 1993; Dressler 1993; Jackson 1993). Barbee's thirty years of nursing experience led her to analyze the "deeply entrenched traditions" of racism in her profession and served as the vantage point against which to evaluate the usefulness of anthropological theory to such an enterprise (Barbee 1993a:324; 1993b).

Rayna Rapp (1990, 1993, 1995), who has studied a cytogenetics laboratory providing prenatal diagnostic testing as part of a metropolitan health department, and Ellen Lazarus (1988, 1990, 1994), who has studied an urban public ob/gyn clinic, have both drawn upon their experiences as anthropologists in drawing conclusions about reproductive health and health policy, as well as about what these culturally loaded settings reveal about the intersections of gender, race, class, and the work of reproducing kin. The balancing of theory and praxis, I contend, lends substance to such analyses.

Participants in applied settings operate both as informants and collaborators whose insights are crucial to the conceptualization and ultimately to the success of the projects thus undertaken (van Willigen, 1993:100–12). This point has been amply illustrated through the work of Helen Lewis and her associates (Lewis and O'Donnell 1990a, 1990b; Hinsdale, Lewis, and Waller 1995), as well as in the work of Steve Fisher (1993), and Richard Couto (1975, 1986, 1993), whose writings attest to the collective wisdom of communities and community-based organizations in Appalachia and their contributions to contemporary analyses of the region, as well as to specific projects of community development and/or social change (White 1993).

Through the Harlem Birthright Project, Leith Mullings and colleagues have organized a collective undertaking that has engaged the expertise of the New York Urban League and representatives from the myriad constituencies of Central Harlem in collaboration with a team of ethnographers who themselves have multiple ties to Harlem (Mullings 1994; Wali, Oliver, and Prince 1994). To address problems of increasing rates of infant mortality in Central Harlem, the project has developed an expanded social network within which to examine issues of pregnancy and access to care and, in so doing, has led to a reexamination of what it means to do urban ethnography. My point is that such alignments of constituencies with multiple forms of local knowledge—some of them strictly or "merely" anthropological—revitalize the discipline and at least potentially serve as the leading edge of anthropological theory.

Let me emphasize that I make no such grand claims for the work presented here. But I will illustrate the ways that informants/collaborators in my research have helped or forced me to revise analyses of gender and activism, and have contributed significantly to my anthropological education as well as to national debates about women's health.

This essay concerns my work over the past three years as a southern anthropologist engaged in field research on breast cancer and breast cancer activism in northern California. I intended to study the ways in which women and their health care providers negotiate treatment decisions in instances of complicated or poor prognosis breast cancer diagnoses; I was not initially concerned with cancer activists per se. Nevertheless, community forums and local media made me aware of the breast cancer community and I began to talk with members of one particular organization about my research interests. I am not sure who recruited whom, although I remember being queried early on about my intentions and personal experience with breast cancer. I remember hearing personal narratives of diagnosis and its aftermath, and I also learned a great deal from the wealth of knowledge accumulated by breast cancer activists through biomedical research as well as bodily experience. The clinical setting, which had been my point of departure, receded into the background.

When I began my research, the group I will refer to as "NORCAL" was barely two years old. The organization had already lost to metastatic breast cancer one of its founding members, a major force in defining the agenda for this grassroots group. The crisis of recurrent and metastatic breast cancer was to prove a dominant theme, which was visited time and again in the fluctuating health and death of the membership and which added to the sense of urgency marking the group's activities.

This predominantly white, middle-class organization had a core constituency of eight women who made up a working board that engaged in many activities. Among other things, representatives from the group testified at scientific meetings and federal hearings, wrote letters to the editors of national and local papers, and spoke at rallies on both coasts. The organization also fielded phone calls and engaged in alliances with women with breast cancer across the country.

When I first came to know NORCAL, the organization was in a period of expansion, having just located the funding to secure office space and launch a series of new activities. A primary objective at that time was to locate able-bodied volunteers to aid in the work of the organization and offset the problem of a membership whose energies were sapped by ongoing struggle, in bodily as well as political terms, with breast cancer. To render this exercise more efficient and useful, the board established six projects that reflected priorities of the grassroots group and in which the labor of volunteers could be easily harnessed.

It is to one of these projects that I will refer: the survey committee. The purpose of this committee was to draft a survey to assess women's experiences of diagnosis and initial treatment for breast cancer. The committee was set up to determine the subject matter to be covered by the questionnaire and the logistics of how and to whom the survey would be administered.

I heard about the survey committee at the beginning of my association with NORCAL. One might say that I was drafted at the outset. It made sense: I was a postdoc in medical anthropology and presumably had skills as well as time to put to the project. Moreover, one of the first people I met in the breast cancer organization was the chair and driving force behind this committee.

In part, the commitment of the chair reflected firsthand experience with the problematics of diagnostic procedures. Equally significant as impetus for the project were phone calls and letters to NORCAL by women who believed their cases to have been poorly handled by "the medical people," to quote one letter. Referring to friends for whom diagnosis of breast cancer had been delayed due to physicians' advice "to wait and watch," the writer urged NORCAL to survey women on their experiences with providers. "If I know five women who have neglected to act for a variety of reasons," she asked, "how many more could be saved?" It is indicative of the power of such correspondence to serve as motivating factor and/or rhetorical device that copies of this letter were distributed to the newly drafted members of the survey committee as well as to the board. Such strategies clarified the mission of the committee.

I want to jump ahead of the story and spoil its punch line: the survey never happened. In that sense, this applied project was an unqualified failure. But a lot happened along the way—a lot of hard, reflective work—which was of immense value to my understanding of this organization and its commitments. I also contend that the survey committee was successful in further educating its own members, members of the NORCAL board, *perhaps,* the broader membership of the organization, and certainly this anthropologist about how to set aside the polemics and seriously think through the implications of this heated issue. These were modest achievements, but achievements nonetheless.

The chair of the survey committee had been shrewd in her recruitment strategies. To supplement the research skills and experiential knowledge of women with breast cancer, she used the services of survey researchers, a statistician, and others from the corporate sector, as well as an anthropologist/university-based researcher. Committee members from the business world brought considerable expertise in quantitative research, as well as the resources of their corporations, including access to computers and computer processors, travel funds enabling one member to attend a cancer research meeting on the East Coast, and the possibility of corporate sponsorship to fund other aspects of the research. As the university researcher, I represented academic credibility. My role was to help the committee formulate a coherent research agenda, develop survey questions that were neither too leading nor too vague to address the underlying hypotheses, and generate a reasonable, if not random, sample. In other words, I was to keep the group on track with respect to issues of bias and validity in the findings of the committee. Finally, the two committee members with breast cancer brought to the undertaking detailed information about diagnostic processes, prognostic indicators, surgical procedures, and therapeutic regimens. They contributed both clinical information and personal insights to the committee.

The activities of the survey committee might be viewed as a long-term negotiation between the seemingly opposite dimensions of personal relevance and scientific validity. In effect, we were attempting to translate the clinical experiences of women with breast cancer into a research document that would be judged as tenable and compelling by policy makers, biomedical researchers, clinicians, and the growing ranks of women at risk for or newly diagnosed with breast cancer. This was, to say the least, a daunting task. The initial statement of our research agenda came from the chair of the survey committee. Based on her activities as recording secretary for NORCAL and as a breast cancer activist in northern California, she presented the work of the committee as documenting the fact that women were receiving negligent care from their physicians. Negotiations were to begin from that premise. My response as a social science researcher and budding epidemiologist was to argue that while such a statement might be validated by letters and phone calls to NORCAL, the survey committee had to design a research project responsive to the *full range* of women's encounters with clinical settings, lest our research endeavor be dismissed as hopelessly biased by the audience we wanted to reach.

For similar reasons, we reexamined our ideas about who the potential survey respondents were to be. We originally planned to target the readers of the NORCAL newsletter, but doing so would mean a base of two thousand women to whom the surveys would be sent. There was, however, a problem of perceived bias in such a sample. If the newsletter readers were mostly women who had experienced difficulties either in the diagnosis or treatment of breast cancer, would our survey not

simply reflect the skewed character of NORCAL's membership/reader-
ship, rather than the pervasiveness of problems in clinical care?

Having participated in forums with medical school faculty, the committee chair was well aware of this issue. Those of us who worked in
research argued for a population-based sample; however, the dilemma
we quickly faced was one of access. How would we reach women who
had been diagnosed with breast cancer, but were neither activists nor
public about their diagnoses? Cancer registries had no interest in making
their databases available to a research group affiliated with a grassroots
organization. I was unwilling to draw upon my university connections to
gain access to registry information because of what I considered significant ethical issues—in particular, the problem of having to present the
research project as my own, thus minimizing NORCAL's presence.

We ultimately decided to draw respondents from the broad array
of organizations focused on breast cancer: those offering information,
patient education, and support services to people affected by breast
cancer, as well as grassroots groups organized by women with breast
cancer. This method was still a far cry from a population-based approach, but we would no longer be targeting women who were already
committed to breast cancer activism. Our research objectives changed
from documenting examples of physician negligence to assessing the
range of women's experiences and the type/frequency of problems they
encountered with both diagnosis and treatment. Moreover, we were prepared for examples of providers who illustrated the model course of
actions to be followed from initial discovery of a breast lump through
diagnosis and treatment for breast cancer. The survey would pull together the testimony of women who had been treated for breast cancer
to inform physicians about the needs of their patients and to educate
women as potential patients on how to negotiate the medical system so
as to receive better and more timely care.

In retrospect, I believe the survey was undone by the decision to
broaden its aims and target audience. The scale of the project taxed the
resources of a small working group formed on the principle of volunteer
efforts and the vision of the chair. Moreover, the mission of the committee became obscured by disagreements between the chair and her
colleagues on the NORCAL board on other, unrelated matters. The committee was subsequently dissolved, having run a focus group and drafted
a preliminary questionnaire and research proposal. (Because of difficul-

ties in recruiting participants, only one focus group, rather than four as originally planned, was held.) It was no small irony that after the committee had been dismantled, NORCAL received word that the project had been funded.

The survey committee satisfied neither the requirements for scientific credibility nor the request of the initial letter writer, but it did achieve results. The first is a model of physician practice, mentioned above. Moreover, through a focus group consisting of six white women with various ties to NORCAL, we had some measure of the distance between the idealized model and the care women actually received. Within this small, nonrandom sample were experiences of delayed diagnosis (2 of the 6); miscommunication of test results, overridden after several days' passage with the message of a positive diagnosis of breast cancer (1); and diagnoses delivered over the phone, rather than in person (2). One woman had a completely satisfactory experience with the physician making the initial diagnosis, a story that occasioned much comment. There were also stories of surgeons who gave misinformation about the need for adjuvant (or post-surgical) treatment, an area of care that is properly the concern of oncologists. In at least one instance, a surgeon told a postmenopausal woman that she would receive chemotherapy, advice that is incorrect (Henderson 1991). Physicians in this sample also dismissed women's concerns about bodily changes after surgery by likening mastectomy to the experience of growing a beard and/or telling women that they would adjust.

What stood out in this material was the gulf between the kinds of information women said they received and what they needed, not only to make decisions about treatment but also to chart their course *through* treatment, once decided upon. Two women described the literature provided by the National Cancer Institute as "Dick and Jane happy people" going through the motions, with little mention of the sometimes "bizarre" side effects of chemotherapy. Oncologists and surgeons alike deflected women's concerns about the complications of treatment: test results indicating liver problems; early onset of menopause as the result of chemotherapy; lymphedema as the result of prognostic tests done on lymph nodes. So long as these problems were not directly related to the cancer itself, they were considered to be minor.

Women in the focus group and in NORCAL, on the other hand, wanted to know what to expect and how to minimize or offset the problems associated with treatment. They also wanted to know what to do to prevent or delay recurrence of the cancer, how closely they were to monitor their bodies, and which signs to look for. To their questions and concerns, women received answers such as (I paraphrase), "You want a bone scan? Fine, I'll order it" or "Sure, it can't hurt you to take anti-oxidants [vitamins]. I take them myself." Health care providers in this sample were reluctant to give specific advice, particularly on matters pertaining to disease-free survival. For this kind of information, all the women in the focus group turned to support groups, which proved to be sources of practical knowledge, and to medical libraries. As one of the participants observed, "Each of us had to fight on our own, one way or another. We all tended to be verbal, aggressive readers, but what if we hadn't been?"

I do not want to make too much of the survey committee, but neither do I wish to minimize it. For anthropologists working in applied settings, the ultimate message of the committee is that such collaborations yield results in a context beyond the control of the anthropologist as practitioner/researcher. What must be described in academic terms as a failing, the inability to complete the survey, became an important opportunity to examine the disjuncture between my goals and those of the chair. She wanted the committee to produce credible and legitimate results, but the process of carrying out academically oriented research proved too cumbersome and too distancing from NORCAL's constituency to be feasible. It would have been the survey that swallowed the organization, or at least some of its members.

The "preliminary findings" of the committee were perhaps a slightly more detailed account of the divide that separates "clinical treatment" from "compassionate care," to draw upon the discussion at one of our last meetings. We learned this lesson in terms that were consonant with the origins and current activities of NORCAL. As the chair noted in a prior conversation with me, the question we were really addressing throughout our ten months as committee was: what makes women activists? What prompted middle-aged and older women, with little or no prior involvement in social movements, to come together in protest over breast cancer?

We discovered women's need for concrete information about the disease and its consequences, as well as an alternative to dehumanizing, sometimes substandard, regimens of care. It was for the "we" who were not aggressive readers that activists pressed their case, as well as for the many competent researchers among them who quickly ran through the known literature and current treatments, to little or no avail. What we learned was also meant for those yet to be diagnosed, the much-discussed daughters and granddaughters growing up in a toxic world. To return to the starting point of this essay, these were the committee's answers to Karen Sacks's important question, "What are the issues women find worth fighting about?" (Sacks 1989:543).

REFERENCES

Barbee, Evelyn L. 1993a. Racism and Gender in U.S. Health Care. *Medical Anthropology Quarterly* 7(4):323–24.

————. 1993b. Racism in U.S. Nursing. *Medical Anthropology Quarterly* 7(4):346–62.

Bourdieu, Pierre. 1972. *Outline of a Theory of Practice.* Cambridge: Cambridge University Press.

Clark, Lauren. 1993. Gender and Generation in Poor Women's Household Health Production Experiences. *Medical Anthropological Quarterly* 7(4): 386–402.

Couto, Richard A. 1975. *Poverty, Politics, and Health Care: An Appalachian Experience.* New York: Praeger.

————. 1986. Failing Health and New Prescriptions: Community-based Approaches to Environmental Risks. In *Current Health Policy Issues and Alternatives,* ed. Carole E. Hill, pp. 53–70. Athens: University of Georgia Press.

————. 1993. The Memory of Miners and the Conscience of Capital: Coal Miners' Strikes as Free Spaces. In *Fighting Back in Appalachia,* ed. Stephen L. Fisher, pp. 165–94. Philadelphia: Temple University Press.

Dressler, William W. 1993. Health in the African American Community: Accounting for Health Inequalities. *Medical Anthropology Quarterly* 7(4): 325–45.

Fisher, Stephen L. 1993. New Populist Theory and the Study of Dissent in Appalachia. In *Fighting Back in Appalachia,* ed. Stephen L. Fisher, pp. 339–60. Philadelphia: Temple University Press.

Henderson, I. Craig. 1991. Adjuvant Systemic Therapy of Early Breast Cancer. In *Breast Diseases,* ed. Jay R. Harris, Samuel Hellman, I. Craig Henderson, and David W. Kinne, pp. 427–86. Philadelphia: J. B. Lippincott.

Hinsdale, Mary Ann, Helen M. Lewis, and S. Maxine Waller. 1995. *It Comes from the People: Community Development and Local Theology.* Philadelphia: Temple University Press.

Jackson, Eileen M. 1993. Whiting-Out Difference: Why U.S. Nursing Research Fails Black Families. *Medical Anthropology Quarterly* 7(4):363–85.

Lazarus, Ellen S. 1988. Poor Women, Poor Outcomes: Social Class and Reproductive Health. In *Childbirth in America: Anthropological Perspectives,* ed. Karen L. Michaelson, pp. 39–54. South Hadley, MA: Bergin and Garvey.

———. 1990. Falling through the Cracks: Contradictions and Barriers to Care in a Prenatal Clinic. *Medical Anthropology* 12:269–87.

———. 1994. What Do Women Want?: Issues of Choice, Control, and Class in Pregnancy and Childbirth. *Medical Anthropology Quarterly* 8(1):25–46.

Lewis, Helen M., and Suzanna O'Donnell, eds. 1990a. *Ivanhoe, Virginia: Remembering Our Past, Building Our Future.* Ivanhoe, VA: Ivanhoe Civic League.

———. 1990b. *Telling Our Stories, Sharing Our Lives.* Ivanhoe, VA: Ivanhoe Civic League.

Mullings, Leith P. 1994. Reevaluating Perspectives on the American Family. Paper presented at the annual meeting of the American Anthropological Association, Atlanta, GA.

Rapp, Rayna. 1990. Constructing Amniocentesis: Maternal and Medical Discourses. In *Uncertain Terms: Negotiating Gender in American Culture,* ed. Faye Ginsburg and Anna Tsing, pp. 28–42. Boston: Beacon Press.

———. 1993. Accounting for Amniocentesis. In *Knowledge, Power, and Practice: The Anthropology of Medicine and Everyday Life,* ed. Shirley Lindenbaum and Margaret Lock pp. 55–76. Berkeley and Los Angeles: University of California Press.

———. 1995. Risky Business: Genetic Counseling in a Shifting World. In *Articulating Hidden Histories: Exploring the Influence of Eric R. Wolf,* ed. Jane Schneider and Rayna Rapp, pp. 175–89. Berkeley and Los Angeles: University of California Press.

Sacks, Karen Brodkin. 1989. Toward a Unified Theory of Class, Race, and Gender. *American Ethnologist* 16:534–50.

van Willigen, John. 1993. *Applied Anthropology: An Introduction.* Westport, CT: Bergin and Garvey.

Wali, Alaka, Denise R. Oliver, and Saibhya Robin Prince. 1994. Harlem Birthright: Redefining Health through a New Approach to Urban Ethnography. Paper presented at the annual meeting of the American Anthropological Association, Atlanta, GA.

White, Connie. 1993. Fighting Back in Appalachia: Reports from the Front. Paper presented at the plenary session of the annual meeting of the Appalachian Studies Association, Johnson City, TN.

Barriers and Opportunities for Practicing Anthropology in the Mississippi Delta (and Getting Paid to Do It)

S. Bridget Ciaramitaro

In 1981, I received an M.A. degree in anthropology from the University of Memphis. This program was created to prepare students to practice anthropology outside of academia. Skills gained in this program provided the basis for realizing a unique career path in community empowerment and economic development. This path led to the creation of a consulting, training, and research business that takes the practice of anthropology into neighborhoods, community development corporations, hospitals, churches, and a variety of work settings. In this essay, I focus on activities and processes of skill development, career visioning, goal setting, and the practice of anthropology, all of which have resulted in rewarding and profitable work as well as an opportunity to contribute to the discipline of anthropology.

APPLIED ANTHROPOLOGY AND CONSULTING

In December 1990, I left a department of anthropology to begin a consulting business that focuses on leadership development and empowerment of individuals, groups, businesses, and institutions in the Lower Mississippi Delta region. Many of the products offered by Ciaramitaro & Associates have been developed using anthropological research conducted in the Delta. These products include:

- A leadership program that empowers older citizens to remain independent and in control of their lives

- Community-based leadership programs that empower residents to define their own goals and develop effective strategies to take charge of community improvements
- Assistance to nonprofit organizations in the areas of visioning board and staff development, responding to changes in economic realities, etc.
- Employee and management training programs that empower staff to implement total quality initiatives and improve communications within the institutional culture
- Skill development in team approaches to conflict resolution and negotiation
- Ongoing research that follows the evolution of regional culture.

BECOMING A PRACTICING ANTHROPOLOGIST

I will now discuss the path I took to become a practicing anthropologist and the ways in which I have built and maintained a viable business.

When I received my undergraduate degree in anthropology in 1973, there were no graduate programs available that encouraged the practice of anthropology outside the university. All my undergraduate education was offered in an environment of defining "real" anthropologists as people who received Ph.D.'s, completed dissertations in cultures outside North America, and eventually landed positions in universities teaching others to follow the same route. I resisted this route because I could not see how advanced degrees in traditional anthropology would help me realize my personal goal of returning to the Delta and making a difference in the region's social and economic struggles.

I was very skeptical when the University of Memphis began discussing the applied M.A. There was nothing about the way it was presented that sounded like anything I had heard in the course of my undergraduate education. I enrolled in the program as a means of buying time until I could identify a career path.

Within two weeks I was hooked. The tension in the department at that time between the traditional anthropologists and those trying to implement the applied master's was stimulating. I was able to witness the struggle in the discipline of anthropology in microcosm in the department. Our heated discussions made it apparent that there was more to anthropology than I had been led to believe.

I gradually began to realize that as an anthropologist I could make a difference in issues of culture change and economic redistribution in the Delta South. This direct access to the evolving dialogue was as important as the skills and theory that were presented. I was encouraged to be a critical thinker about the discipline, the region, institutions, and culture change. This was a major breakthrough as I moved from student of anthropology to an empowered practitioner. For three years I lived, breathed, and worked anthropology. I took on many different jobs in research and application while also completing course work. It never occurred to me that doing so would not lead to a productive, somewhat financially secure career path, but I also knew that it would be a path that in the long run I would have to make for myself.

As part of the required practicum experience, I held an internship in a local nonprofit development organization where I was encouraged to share my anthropological insights into issues they were addressing. Although I was tense, scared, and unsure of my abilities, I did not back off. I began to define for the agency, and for myself, the interface of anthropology and development.

As I moved toward graduation in 1981, I was given an opportunity to continue dialogue and experimentation. Within the department we had begun a discussion of setting up a research center that would focus on community and economic development in the Delta. The Center for Voluntary Action Research was funded by First Tennessee Bank. If anthropologists could be colleagues with bankers, anything was possible.

This funding provided an open door for me to remain affiliated with the university after graduation while continuing to work on applied projects. In my role as co-director of this new center I faced one last stumbling block planted deeply in my cognitive map during my undergraduate education: could anyone really be an anthropologist and not have a Ph.D.?

ROLE MODELS FOR PRACTICING ANTHROPOLOGY

There were to my knowledge no models of successful anthropologists who had not completed a Ph.D. By the time I was facing this question, I had played a leadership role in several successful nontraditional applied projects, two of which eventually earned WAPA's International Praxis awards. When I talked with faculty in Ph.D. programs, however, there was an overwhelming message—if you want to become one of us, you are going to have to be reprogrammed and it is going to take a long, long, long time, not to mention a lot of money. The final blow came when I traveled a thousand miles to a university for an interview and the chair of the graduate program spent half of the thirty minutes he had allotted me making theater reservations over the telephone!

Through WAPA and SfAA I discovered that there were indeed models of M.A.-level anthropologists making a contribution to the discipline to universities and to the outside world as well. Robert Wulff and Anthony DiBella were particularly instrumental in creating a path for anthropologists with M.A.'s. Therefore, I decided not to pursue a Ph.D.

After completing the M.A., I worked in the Department of Anthropology at the University of Memphis for nine years, during which time I gained experience in directing research and development programs in the Delta South. Rather than seeing each project as a "quick and dirty" effort, I began building the various projects into a broad understanding of regional culture. My experience brought me into contact with a wide range of clients from utility companies to banks to neighborhood associations. The many research projects we conducted helped me to identify and understand barriers to empowerment of community-based leaders and obstacles to changing the traditional leadership structure in the society of the Delta.

In 1988, I began seriously to consider leaving the university. Dealing with the internal institutional roadblocks became more and more frustrating. I was uncertain, however, what effect leaving the university might have on my credibility. How important was my institutional affiliation in expanding my network of clients?

Many entrepreneurs have experienced a dramatic change in the workplace that served to jolt them into making a change in their circumstances. So it was with me as I faced the challenge of practicing anthropology without an institutional affiliation. In the fall of 1990, the department chair who developed the applied M.A. program left his position and returned to the faculty. In the face of a major recession and the Desert Storm conflict, I left the university and began Ciaramitaro & Associates. I have never looked back or regretted this decision, although starting a business is difficult. I experienced firsthand why it is important to have six months' income in the bank. But I was pleasantly surprised to make these discoveries:

- Being an anthropologist who could offer anthropological skills through the products discussed in the beginning of this essay was an asset in expanding my client base.
- Being away from the university was also seen as positive by many clients. It was now possible to expedite activities.
- A market was in place for the products I was developing.
- It was possible to make a living doing what I really wanted to do.

CRITICAL FACTORS IN PRACTICING ANTHROPOLOGY OUTSIDE THE UNIVERSITY

Successfully practicing anthropology outside the university, like other professions, depends on communication skills, ability to deal with the stress of uncertainty, maintenance of flexibility, and involvement with diverse people. Activities such as assessing the need for office space, expanding computer and other tools and accessories, keeping accurate financial records, and hiring and firing staff are all necessary but at the same time distracting to the delivery of quality products to clients.

In the last four and one-half years I have come to appreciate a number of things that I know paved the way for my current career satisfaction:

- The foresight of those whose vision it was to train practitioners for nontraditional careers in anthropology.
- The quality of the M.A.-level education that I received in the Department of Anthropology at the University of Memphis.
- The department's ability to include students in the debate over the issues of theory versus practice and traditional versus nontraditional career paths, thus challenging us to take responsibility for the future of the discipline.
- The leadership of my colleagues outside the university who have stood up to a sometimes hostile discipline and have continued to make contributions.

Reflections of an "Outsider" Anthropologist

Christopher H. Walker

The title of this essay was inspired, in part, by an exhibition at the North Carolina Museum of Art some years ago entitled "Outsider Art." It featured the work of several artists who were considered "outsiders" to the profession in which they found some success. I find myself in the position of being outside of the profession for which I was professionally trained, and an outsider to the vocation in which I am self-trained. Although I received a Ph.D. in anthropology, I am currently in the computer software publishing trade. I have, over the years, written technical documentation as well as designed, developed, and tested software. While little in our current economic climate is "stable," computer and writing skills have allowed me to be adaptable. Far from being unique, my situation as an "outsider" is becoming more common among university-trained anthropologists. In this essay, I discuss some of the issues, both fair and foul, that both current and potential anthropologists have to address.

I entered graduate school in the fall of 1977 and took the traditional ten years to complete the degree. Like everyone else, I was sure that I would be done in five. I was an anthropology major as an undergraduate, but after graduation had an interlude of five years of work and travel before returning to graduate school. The decision to return was based, in part, on missing the intellectual stimulation of the academy and, I now know, on a somewhat romanticized version of professorship. In fact, as I believe is often the case, I knew very little about what graduate school was and even less about survival of the fittest in the academic world. Unless we have parents who are graduate school veterans, we usually know nothing about the academic process until we are already in the middle of it. It only then becomes clear how tortured it can be, not to mention the fact that it is not "job training" at all. With rare exceptions, there is no institutionalized instruction in teaching techniques and organization, public speaking, writing in a comprehensible manner, or obtaining grants. It is an endeavor in research, and if it is acceptable research, written in even marginal prose, it will usually earn the candidate a degree, after which that candidate, left to his or her own devices, will be thrust upon the job market for academic positions, often never having taught a course, there to compete with several hundred of his or her peers for every single position.

Most of us who were students in the late 1970s were told of the surfeit of jobs coming in the mid to late 1980s. Professors would retire, positions would open up, and, unskilled as we were, we would work through these opportunities, as assistant professors have been doing for years, perhaps making respectable researchers and teachers out of ourselves in the process. We know now that this projection did not come to pass except for a small percentage of freshly minted Ph.D.'s The jobs did not open up; in fact, they tightened up, and wonderfully qualified people who had taught courses well, written well, and already had a considerable list of publications, were nowhere close to having interviews. At best, they were taking one-year positions with no benefits and no guarantee of future employment.

A recent newspaper article focused on the proliferation of "part-timers," Ph.D.-holders who assemble as many part-time courses as possible in order to survive while hoping for the "big break." A quotation from one five-year commuting veteran is telling: "In one day I drive 100 miles and teach 100 students at three different colleges. I feel like this information machine, sort of Teach 'R' Us. What are we doing in our cars, all these Ph.D.'s on the freeways?" (Mydans 1995:G5). Friends from my graduate school cohort can certainly attest to driving many more than one hundred miles to earn what often amounts to a poverty-level wage. In addition, any hope of raising a family in a single location for more than one year at a time is a pipe dream for many who would like to have some stability in their lives. Perhaps, then, we will be allowed to read with a skeptical eye a report from the U.S. Census Bureau, entitled "More Education Means Higher Career Earnings" (U.S. Census Bureau

1994). It outlines the average yearly earnings of persons eighteen years or older by level of education for 1992, as follows:

Professional degree	$74,560	Associate degree	$24,398
Doctorate	$54,904	Some college	$19,666
Master's degree	$40,368	High school graduate	$18,737
Bachelor's degree	$32,629	Non-high school	$12,809

Pretty impressive: $54,904 for a doctorate. Of course, it is an average, and includes our colleagues "across the aisle," so to speak, in the natural sciences, in medical schools, and in law and business schools. Many unemployed and underemployed anthropologists are now earning, on a precarious basis, at a level somewhere between no degree and an associate degree.

And what of the "practicing anthropologists," our colleagues who have chosen the "applied" areas of our discipline? My definition of applied anthropology is that it is the practical use of anthropological knowledge, regardless of the subfield with which it is associated. Thus, as long as there are roadways to be built and land to be developed, the archeologists can fall back on "survey and salvage" projects. Although many might prefer the academic setting, excavating in the field is, at least in part, what they were trained to do. If a physical anthropologist uses his or her knowledge to assist the medical examiner, or a cultural anthropologist designs a program to ease tension between an indigenous people and a corporate developer, then it is applied or "practiced" anthropology. A glance at the range of titles for the essays in this symposium illustrates the diversity of topics to which we can apply anthropological knowledge.

Perhaps, then, the applied path in the nonacademic world is the way to income, benefits, and stability. The "real world" outside of the ivory tower beckons with the promise of mammon and the end to indentured servitude as a part-timer. Not quite. A company for which I worked changed managerial hands three times and summarily terminated the employment of one-fourth of the staff with five hours' notice—clear out your desks and don't come back tomorrow. "Downsizing," an odious euphemism, is the watchword of today's economy. Despite the protestations of many economists that it is ultimately demoralizing, unproductive, and a waste of human resources, it is, nevertheless, a current trend. In business, if one has to choose between cutting the positions of the Ph.D.'s and the M.B.A.'s, the Ph.D.'s will usually be the least favored. The business world, however, is at least somewhat more forthright about how tentative one's chances are than is the academic establishment.

Despite appearances to the contrary, all of the foregoing doom and gloom is not a prelude to my advising students to forget graduate school and teaching, and go get the M.B.A. It is, rather, a caveat to potential graduate students to go into the enterprise with their eyes fully open, and a protest to graduate schools and departments to look beyond the body count of Ph.D.'s graduated so that they can truly advise candidates as to whether or not they should invest five to ten years of their lives in a process that makes most of them less, not more, employable. Living on the joy of knowledge and the excitement of research, applied or theoretical, is like living on love—sooner or later the landlord comes to collect. Of what use, then, is this endeavor?

The hallmark of the cultural subfield of the discipline, fieldwork, forces the whole being into action. My graduate advisor aptly described it by saying that one becomes a full-time person, particularly in the case of international fieldwork. There is not any time when one's guard is down. I consider myself to be a cultural anthropologist by predilection since my interest in travel and in learning firsthand about other people preceded my decision to pursue an intellectual and theoretical examination of why we do what we do. Some colleagues, however, appear to suffer the fieldwork only in order to vindicate their theoretical framework. Entering graduate school only to talk the talk will not sustain most pilgrims to the end of the walk. If nothing else, the anthropologist must learn to exploit the adaptability that we tout as the hallmark of human evolution.

All of those hours in the field being a full-time person should make us pretty good listeners. That is, after all, what we are in the field to do. If it is not our inclination, it at least needs to become a practical skill. Quiet listening is never wasted. In a foreign, academic, or corporate culture, listening, beyond making the stay in that culture more enjoyable, can be as essential to survival as eating the green grubs instead of the brown ones. The brashest M.B.A. climbing to the top of the proverbial ladder will, in fact, often not hear the sounds of his or her own impending expulsion from that culture, or at the least, will be clueless as to why the going is rough. Thus, the value of the field experience is not limited to academic research alone.

In addition to listening, adaptability can express itself through self-acquired knowledge, in my case, that of computing. Because I have an aptitude for understanding things technological, I went about this task with gusto at a time when microcomputers were still in the bloom of youth. To some degree, my knowledge kept pace with their development and I suddenly had a marketable skill that allowed me both to help support myself in graduate school and to supplement my income while accompanying my wife overseas for her fieldwork. It is what ultimately allowed me to be gainfully employed as the potential for tenure track faculty positions rapidly dwindled. If I had been flipping burgers during those years instead of increasing my computer skills, my outlook for the future would have been far different. There are usually a number of opportunities available during graduate school for those willing to look for them, opportunities that may later prove to have very practical value.

Another benefit deriving from my anthropological experience was a renewed fondness for literature. I am confident that it is still true today that graduate students in the field for the first time read more novels then than at almost any other time in life. Many professional writers say that the key to developing their writing is a voracious appetite for reading. I therefore contend that, far from feeling guilty about reading *Lolita* in the field rather than those ten back issues of *American Anthropologist,* we should hope that commerce with the best crafters of the language would influence the writing of social scientists in a positive way. I currently write technical manuals for computer software, a far cry from monographs on the symbolic elements of ritual among black Pentecostals in the Caribbean, my dissertation topic. I enjoy writing about both topics because I enjoy making words make sense; however, the income from the technical manuals is steadier. Clear writing, like quiet listening, will never be a detriment.

Could even the arcane inquiries of someone like me who studies the anthropology of symbols be construed as constituting a basis for practicing anthropology? Ritual and symbol are as important in the culture of business, or academia for that matter, as in any other culture. IBM and Apple Corporation have both achieved overwhelming success, but mistake the rituals of one for the other and your stay in that culture will be short-lived. Symbols are not only theoretical constructs but also, as Geertz notes, integral parts of the everyday reality of culture (Geertz 1973). Recognizing them—indeed, analyzing them, in whatever culture one finds oneself—is a key to understanding and operating in that culture. My Ph.D. was of negligible value to my employers when I secured my first job in the software industry, but some of the skills acquired in obtaining that degree served me well.

To faculty members who must advise potential graduate students, I would say recognize the bleakness of the employment situation and be honest about it. Discourage students, tell them that their chances of landing a tenure track job right out of graduate school, and in fact making tenure, are as good as the average high-schooler's chances of making the NBA. To those with applied aspirations, let them know that money is tight and that while practicing anthropology may seem to offer more opportunities, it is fraught with all the perils of a tightening economy.

On the other hand, if what excites these budding anthropologists is the perspective that anthropology brings, if they understand that adaptability both during the graduate process and after it is paramount, then let them know how personally rewarding the process can be. Let them know that the anthropological perspective can enrich their lives no matter how they earn a living. If what comes out of this endeavor is not just a degree, but a new perspective on human life and how we go about living it, along with some practical skills for maintaining ourselves, then they should pursue it with vigor.

REFERENCES

Geertz, Clifford. 1973. *The Interpretation of Cultures.* New York: Basic Books.
Mydans, Seth. 1995. Ph.D. Doesn't Assure a Chair. [Durham, NC] *Herald-Sun* January 8:G5, G8.
U.S. Census Bureau. 1994. *More Education Means Higher Earnings.* Washington, DC: U.S. Census Bureau.

Social Marketing and Applied Anthropology: A Practitioner's View of the Similarities and Differences between Two Research-Driven Disciplines

Christopher A. Brown

In an effort to create consumer-oriented social service programs, government agencies are turning to social marketing. Social marketing is a social change strategy based on a commitment to create products that consumers want as well as need. It draws upon the principles of marketing to influence voluntary behavior in target audiences. It also draws heavily on behavior analysis, education, communications, and anthropology. This essay focuses on the similarities, and mentions some of the differences, between applied anthropology and social marketing, and between social marketing and two models of applied anthropology: the culture broker and action anthropology models.

In my previous job with a nonprofit social marketing firm, Best Start, and in my current job as social marketing specialist with the Bureau of Nutrition Services in the Texas Department of Health, I have had an opportunity to observe the relationship between social marketing and applied anthropology. Examples from my experience with two social marketing projects will illustrate the similarities between the disciplines. The first project was conducted on behalf of the Texas Special Supplemental Nutrition Program for Women, Infants, and Children (WIC), part of the national program by the same name, that provides nutrition education and supplemental foods to low-income women and their children. The second project was conducted for the Texas Interagency Council on Early Childhood Intervention (ECI), the agency in

Texas responsible for administering Part H of the Individuals with Disabilities Education Act. Part H calls for the provision of comprehensive services to families of children with developmental delays who are between birth and three years old. This essay concludes with a discussion of graduate training that would benefit those who want to become practicing anthropologists in the world of social marketing.

SOCIAL MARKETING DEFINED

Social marketing is a social change strategy that combines education, mass communications, and applied behavioral sciences to promote changes that are in the public's interest. At the heart of social marketing is a commitment to understand and respond to clients' needs.

For a program to be called social marketing, it must do three things: use technology from commercial marketing; seek as its bottom line to influence voluntary behavior; and have as a primary goal to help the target audience or society as a whole, rather than the organization conducting the program. It is the application of commercial marketing technologies that truly sets social marketing apart from other, similar disciplines, such as health communication and social advertising, with which social marketing is sometimes confused (Andreason 1994).

THE SOCIAL MARKETING PROCESS

The social marketing process is a cycle with six stages: formative research, strategy formation, program development, program implementation, monitoring and revision, and evaluation. Once the process is complete, it begins anew.

FORMATIVE RESEARCH

Literature reviews, participant observation, in-depth interviews, focus groups, and surveys are among the data collection techniques used during formative research. Data drive the entire social marketing process. Social marketers seek to identify: the motives and barriers to adopting or not adopting certain behaviors; the knowledge, attitudes, practices, values, and beliefs that affect behavior; the marketing messages that may be most effective for influencing behavior; the most effective communication channels for delivering messages; and the audience segments (e.g., Anglo, African American, Hispanic) that may need to be differentially targeted with marketing messages. In some cases, research is also conducted among staff of the agency for whom the study is conducted.

STRATEGY FORMATION

Once formative research is complete, data are used to develop strategies for carrying out the goals of the program. During strategy development, researchers present their findings, and a collaborative process, usually a series of meetings, begins. The meetings involve researchers, agency staff on whose behalf the study was conducted, and policy makers. Their goal is to identify strategies that will be most effective for influencing voluntary behavior of target audiences. Policy changes, either within the agency itself or made by legislative bodies, that will augment strategies are also identified. These strategies serve as the basis for a social marketing plan, which entails a specific set of goals, objectives, and strategies for carrying out external (e.g., target audiences outside the agency) and, if needed, internal (e.g., target audiences within the agency) communication campaigns.

PROGRAM DEVELOPMENT AND IMPLEMENTATION

During program development, the social marketing plan is refined, and marketing messages and materials are designed and pretested for effectiveness. The social marketing plan serves as the guidepost for implementing the social marketing program. Pilot projects are a typical feature of program implementation when the program will eventually be executed over a large geographic area, such as a state. Strategies are implemented on a small scale to identify strengths and weaknesses before carrying the program to scale.

MONITORING, REVISION, AND EVALUATION

Finally, the program is monitored, revised, and evaluated. If evaluation results indicate a need for major changes, the process begins again.

The hallmark of social marketing is its consumer-based, research-driven focus. Social marketers consult consumers for their "expert" testimony throughout the social marketing process. Strategies are developed based on what the users and potential users of a product (commodity, idea, or behavior) want and need. Target audience segments with different marketing messages, based on social and cultural differences among the segments, are determined. Products are positioned to be nonthreatening; they are placed for convenience and their costs to the consumer are reduced. As a result of the consumer focus of social marketing, it is the product and the organization delivering the product that often must change the most and not the consumer. Kotler and Roberto (1989:26) eloquently summarize this view: "Social marketing is built around . . . the setting of measurable objectives, research on human needs, targeting products to specialized groups of consumers, the technology of positioning products to fit consumer needs and wants and effectively communicating their benefits, the constant vigilance to changes in the environment, and the ability to change and adapt."

ANTHROPOLOGY'S CONTRIBUTION TO SOCIAL MARKETING

The social marketer looks to anthropology for an understanding of the cultural context in which a social marketing program will be implemented, and to ensure that marketing messages and materials are culturally appropriate. To better understand the knowledge, attitudes, practices, values, and beliefs of target audiences, social marketers use participant observation and in-depth interviewing along with focus group interviewing and surveys. The ways anthropologists use to record, analyze, and report qualitative data are applied by social marketers. In addition, ethnographies written about a target audience often provide a rich source of secondary data that helps to inform the social marketing process, particularly during formative research (Smith 1989).

Kotler and Andreason (1991:420) also point out that anthropology helps social marketers identify the barriers and motivators to prohibiting, modifying, or adopting behaviors. They go on to say that anthropology contributes by: "1) helping to identify likely 'early adopters' of specific new behaviors; 2) learning how the behavior change can best be constructed to maximize adoption . . . ; 3) showing what words, phrases, and images are appropriate to describe the behavior change so that its benefits are clearly understood and the change advocated is as non-threatening as possible; and 4) helping to select and train change agents who can be most empathetic and effective in a given 'foreign' culture" (1991:420–21).

SOCIAL MARKETING AND APPLIED ANTHROPOLOGY

Social marketing and applied anthropology have much in common. In an effort to promote social change or stability, both use complementary qualitative and quantitative data collection techniques to develop research-driven strategies for direct action and/or policy development.

John van Willigen (1986:8) defines applied anthropology as "a complex of related, research-based, instrumental methods which produce change or stability in specific cultural systems through the provision of data, initiation of direct action and/or policy." Breaking down this definition into components and using examples from the Texas WIC and ECI projects will illustrate the similarities between social marketing and applied anthropology.

First, social marketing is "a complex of related, research-based instrumental methods." In-depth interviews, focus groups, a door-to-door survey, and a statewide survey were used to collect data during the ECI project. A primary goal of formative research was to find ways to define hard-to-reach populations. Since the majority of referrals to ECI come from the medical community, ECI officials thought that the hard-to-reach people were likely to be those who do not use pediatric care for their children. In-depth interviews were conducted at various sites where it was possible to access hard-to-reach populations, such as low-income child care centers and other social service agencies. Results revealed that most parents used pediatric care only in acute cases, not for preventive care. This finding was significant because developmental delays are less likely to be identified in children who do not receive preventive care. The hard-to-reach population was therefore termed the "medically hard-to-reach"; the category included parents who never or seldom used preventive pediatric care.

The data from these interviews were used to generate questions for a door-to-door survey conducted in two low-income urban communities, with a primary goal of identifying the percentage of medically hard-to-reach people and determining strategies for reaching them. A statewide survey was conducted that addressed several limitations of the door-to-door survey, such as urban-rural differences. These techniques are related because they were applied systematically. In other words, the data generated from one technique informed the development of instruments used in other techniques.

Second, social marketing involves producing "change or stability in specific cultural systems." Using marketing principles, the social marketer segments the target audience into distinct subgroups based on a number of characteristics (e.g., race, ethnicity, gender, age, behavior). The social marketer uses anthropology to identify the social and/or cultural factors that most influence behavior in different subgroups and uses this information to design messages that will be most effective. In the Texas WIC project, telephone and focus group interviews conducted with women who were eligible for WIC, but not using it, revealed that for some their reluctance or embarrassment to accept government assistance prevented them from enrolling. A statewide survey indicated that when compared to African Americans and Hispanics, a much larger percentage of Anglos think it is embarrassing to use WIC. The survey also found that the proportion of those who think receiving WIC is an embarrassment is higher among women who have received formal education beyond high school, regardless of race (Bryant 1994:28). To influence participation among eligible women, specific messages were developed to remove the stigma associated with program participation. The primary target audience for these messages included Anglos and those women who had formal education beyond high school. While this portion of the overall WIC social marketing plan sought behavior change, some social marketing campaigns seek to stabilize or discourage behavior, such as the "Just Say No" antidrug use campaign in the United States (Andreason 1994:111).

Third, promoting behavior change or the stability of behavior is accomplished "through the provision of direct action and/or the formulation of policy." As noted above, data gathered during the formative research stage are used to develop a comprehensive set of strategic change policies. In many social marketing programs, policy development takes the form of state and national legislation. It also directs changes in the service delivery system. For example, the WIC study revealed that long waits in WIC clinics negatively affected client satis-faction. In fact, 50 percent of clients surveyed say they wait too long in the clinic (Bryant 1994:50). The social marketing plan outlined policy changes to reduce wait times.

Policy is not only an outcome of the social marketing process, but may also be the driving force behind an agency's decision to conduct a social marketing study. If so, the social marketing process itself be-comes a form of direct action. The impetus for the WIC and ECI projects were separate mandates delivered by the U.S. Congress requiring both programs to serve more eligible families. WIC and ECI officials decided to take action by contracting for social marketing studies to determine how best to increase enrollment.

Of course, social marketing is more than applied anthropology, since the organizing principle for problem solving is marketing, not anthro-pology.

SOCIAL MARKETING AND THE MODELS OF APPLIED ANTHROPOLOGY

I have had a wonderful opportunity to practice anthropology. My duties have encompassed every part of the social marketing process. As a result of this experience, I have seen how social marketing overlaps with cer-tain aspects of the culture broker and action anthropology models of applied anthropology. (See van Willigen 1986 for a thorough description of these and other models.)

CULTURE BROKER

Government agencies, realizing that a top-down approach to service delivery is ineffective, have acknowledged the need for individuals who have the means to link them to their consumers. My role in social marketing has most closely resembled that of a culture broker; a me-diator between one culture, the client agency who has contracted for or is engaged in social marketing activities, and a second culture, the consumers of the agency's services. The link is created through con-stant consumer research throughout the social marketing process that drives the development of agency policy, and the creation of strate-gies that will help them sustain the link. This link provides a voice for consumer-directed change in the agency. When combined with the social marketer's knowledge of agency policy and operations, this voice is translated into change strategies that become part of the social marketing plan.

My role as a culture broker is temporary because it is limited to the social marketing process. We have seen how this temporary brokering affected policy concerning waiting times in WIC clinics. The link is being sustained, however, through a Permanent Data Collection System (PDCS) comprised of three surveys, one of which is designed to monitor client satisfaction. The creation of community coalitions is another strategy that is being employed to maintain the link between WIC and its consumers. These coalitions, comprised of individuals and agencies identified through research to be credible sources of information, will be the focus of community-based activities designed to increase WIC enrollment.

Where social marketing diverges from the culture broker model is in its emphasis on behavior change in the target audience. While both approaches target the client agency for change (e.g., service delivery), behavior change in the target audience is not the primary focus of the culture broker model (van Willigen 1986:139). Social marketing programs may seek stability in behavior, but there is a general preference for behavior change; in this way, social marketing begins to resemble action anthropology.

ACTION ANTHROPOLOGY

Social marketing and action anthropology attempt to influence behavior change in target audiences. Both approaches have a strong interactive research component, in which the researcher examines the values of the community to determine program goals and strategies for influencing behavior. Like action anthropology, social marketing seeks through persuasion and education to provide target audiences with the freedom to choose between alternatives—namely choosing to engage or not engage in a particular behavior. In doing so, social marketers attempt to remove the barriers restricting choice.

Data gathered during the ECI project illustrate these similarities. One of the challenges facing ECI is to have more children screened for developmental delays, and this need became a major component of ECI's social marketing plan. Statewide survey data reveal that parents' level of concern that one of their children may have a developmental delay makes them significantly more likely to want to have their children screened. A far greater proportion of parents (84 percent) want their children screened who also say they are concerned when compared to parents who are not concerned (48 percent). Some mothers who participated in focus groups say that they had an instinctive sense that something was wrong with their child. Those who were enrolled in ECI to seek help for their children were motivated by the knowledge that a program existed that could help them act in the best interest of those children. Some parents, however, noted that when they expressed their concerns to their children's pediatricians, the children were misdiagnosed, their concerns were dismissed, or a referral to ECI was delayed (Brown 1994). The social marketing plan recommends educating parents about the availability of screening services, and using concern, the knowledge that parents are not alone in their concern, the desire to do what is best for their children, and listening to their instinctive sense to motivate parents to have their children screened. Encouraging parents to listen to their instinctive sense could also be used to overcome the barrier to enrollment resulting from misdiagnoses, delayed referrals, and dismissed concerns.

The primary goals of social marketing and action anthropology are different. Unlike action anthropology, the goal of social marketing is not to create self-determining communities. Action programs often begin with an intervention in a single domain of behavior. Working with the community, the anthropologist selects a problem to solve where the likelihood of success is high. As success is achieved in one problem area and the community becomes better integrated, interventions can be expanded to more difficult problem areas in the community. The community is eventually able to solve problems on its own. The process works best in the absence of an intervening agency (van Willigen 1986:59–77).

In contrast, social marketers work through an intervening agency that has already selected a problem (e.g., increasing enrollment in WIC). The anthropologist does not work with the community to select a problem, and the process begins and ends with the investigation of a single domain of behavior. We have seen that some social marketing programs create community coalitions to carry out community-based activities, but the goal is not to expand beyond the problem at hand. As long as social marketers contract with government agencies that select problems to be investigated, and that generally operate in a single domain of behavior, it is not likely that the creation of self-determining communities will be a goal of social marketing.

TRAINING PRACTICING ANTHROPOLOGISTS FOR SOCIAL MARKETING CAREERS

Social marketing has a bright future. There is an opportunity for applied anthropologists to fill positions in social marketing firms as well as governmental and nongovernmental organizations who use social marketing. Proper training will be vital to applied anthropologists as they compete for these positions.

In addition to a concentration in applied training on anthropological theory and qualitative and quantitative research methods, training for social marketing careers should include the following:

- Course work in some or all of the disciplines that contribute to social marketing (marketing, communications, education, and behavioral analysis), and in the context in which the anthropologist desires to practice (e.g., public health)
- Oral presentation skills
- Technical report writing
- Differences between research theory and research practice.

CONCLUSIONS

More and more anthropologists, those trained in theoretical and as well as in applied programs, are seeking employment outside academia. There is, however, the danger that employment situations that do not allow anthropologists to use their skills will result in their losing touch with the discipline. To avoid this problem, anthropologists should search for positions that allow them to apply their anthropological knowledge. To help with this search and to add to the body of knowledge about anthropological applications, those who are practicing anthropology should share their experiences. Social marketing is a wonderful opportunity to apply anthropological knowledge to solving real-world problems.

REFERENCES

Andreason, A. 1994. Social Marketing: Its Definition and Domain. *Journal of Public Policy and Marketing* 13:108–14.

Brown, C. 1994. *The Texas ECI Social Marketing Study: Building Program Enrollment through Increased Community Awareness (Phase II Final Report).* Austin: ECI.

Bryant, C. 1994. *WIC at the Crossroads: The Texas WIC Marketing Study.* Austin: Texas Department of Health/Bureau of Nutrition Services.

Kotler, P., and A. Andreason. 1991. *Strategic Marketing for Non-Profit Organizations.* Englewood Cliffs, NJ: Prentice-Hall.

Kotler, P., and E. Roberto. 1989. *Social Marketing: Strategies for Changing Public Behavior.* New York: The Free Press.

Smith, W. 1989. *Lifestyles for Survival: The Role of Social Marketing in Mass Education.* Washington, DC: Academy for Educational Development.

van Willigen, John. 1986. *Applied Anthropology: An Introduction.* South Hadley, MA: Bergin and Garvey.

Applications in the Private Practice of Urban Planning

Michael M. English

In 1974, I enrolled in the first term of the University of South Florida's M.A. program in applied anthropology. My undergraduate degree was in finance and pre-law, and my experience with anthropology course work had been minimal.

My interest in the program was spurred by a *St. Petersburg Times* interview of Ailon Shiloh, then the graduate program director. The article told an enticing story of what was then a new idea—that the powerful analytical tools and perceptual abilities of the discipline could be taught to M.A.-level students, who could then work in modern American settings to become creative and empathetic problem solvers.

Other members of that first cohort, few of whom had any real background in anthropology, were attracted by that same interview, which seemed to hold great promise for a new context in which to apply a social science that was somewhat mysterious to the general public—if you had the nerve to take a chance. A professional degree in anthropology had not occurred to any of us, because of our perception that the field was limited to a doctorate and teaching/research/service. That general perspective was laced with a cautious faith in a new pathway to an M.A. degree and meaningful public service. The faculty responsible for creating the program and teaching it were committed, but unsure of the outcome of their experiment.

Nevertheless, they fit our world view of anthropologists. They shared a special perspective about how life is organized. The program required a rapid immersion into survey courses of the four traditional subfields, which created an initial culture shock for most of us.

The two-year program was designed to move students quickly into the literature, and then offer case study, practicum projects, and research-oriented course work, before the semester-long internship and thesis-writing period. One of the features of the program was the requirement to choose a "track": Urban or Medical Applied Anthropology, or Public Archeology, allowing each student to optimize the use of electives and an internship.

It became apparent that the faculty was reality-testing the curriculum as we went along, and most of the students developed great admiration for them, both for their leadership and teaching ability, and in a sort of mutual pioneer-bonding way.

I initially had difficulty with the reading (probably as a result of too many youthful years of debauchery), and it was only with the help of several faculty members that I made it. The faculty's first urban specialist, Bob Wulff, encouraged me to follow my interest in the urban track early on, seek entry-level employment in the urban planning field, and work while taking course work in the evening (all courses were offered from 6:00 P.M. to 10:00 P.M.).

I followed his advice and the solution worked for me. After beginning with no pay for three months in an effort to become paid staff, I was hired as junior staff at the Hillsborough County Planning Commission, where I worked for five years, while completing graduate studies at a slow pace.

For me, the longer period of exposure to the faculty and graduate program was significant, as I learned more anthropology and became better at integrating anthropological concepts with urban planning practices.

My time as a junior planner/graduate student was also valuable because I was able (thanks to Bob Wulff, and later Erve Chambers) to use anthropological techniques and research models in several of the planning studies and projects I worked on at the Planning Commission, including key informant interviewing, sociocultural surveys in neighborhood planning and demographic analysis, and a constant search for the insiders' perspective in the process of preparing recommendations for changes in land use and zoning in the community.

As I completed all of the required course work, as well as every urban planning elective available at the university, I was offered the position of Planning Director in a small community in the Tampa Bay Area, the City of Safety Harbor. My thesis was based on my job experience as Planning

Director, particularly on the development and adoption of the community's comprehensive plan. My primary challenge was to convince the community to accept the concept of urban planning as a comprehensive self-management tool, albeit one that had been recently legally mandated by the state government. I used key informants, networking concepts, and sleight of hand to convince them to do what I saw as necessary. The result was the successful local adoption of a comprehensive plan.

My extended internship, which took up most of that four- to five-year period during which I was studying anthropology and becoming an urban planner, has shaped my career in many ways. Extended interaction with architects, urban designers, landscape architects, art historians, and practitioners of other related disciplines fostered in me a belief in the multidisciplinary nature of urban design, and the complexity of the disparate cultural values that guide the rise and fall of our society's physical fabric.

After nearly three years in Safety Harbor, I left to work for private-sector land developers, motivated by a desire to learn about the other side of the equation—the regulated entrepreneurs. It was a formative experience, and gave me the opportunity I was seeking to become a developer and observe firsthand how the marketplace interacted in the design, construction, marketing, and sale of the built environment.

From a philosophical perspective, I reached my own conclusions about suburbs and urban sprawl. All of my employer's activity was in the suburbs, and was focused on strip commercial shopping centers and office buildings, and single-family residential development. The experience taught me a great deal and confirmed that my interests were located in cities, and concerned with redevelopment, preservation, and urban infill, all ideas just coming into vogue in Florida.

A recession forced me to look for another job, as my employers downsized their activities. I returned to Tampa and was fortunate to be hired by the development subsidiary of Tampa's largest savings and loan. The year I was there was among the strangest in my career, but I certainly learned a great deal. I worked directly for the company president, and for the first several months just observed him making deals and money.

My real assignment was a surprise. The subsidiary acquired a local real estate sales company—ten offices, 150 sales associates, and large operating losses—and I was sent out to manage the company out of

its severe loss position. It is an understatement to say that I was techni-
cally unprepared. I did not have a real estate license and I had no management experience. I was, however, a practicing anthropologist with
people skills.

I identified the staff who were really running the company, and soon
thereafter, the people obstructing the work flow. For a month I watched
and asked questions. At that point, I recommended that the only way
to stop the operating losses was to downsize, which we did by closing
two-thirds of the offices and releasing the same percentage of sales associates and office staff. For the balance of my time there, the scaled-
down company focused on rebuilding business relationships and selling
homes. When I left, the company was about to break even and I had
again learned a lot.

The recession ended, and I was ready to try developing on my own.
The subsidiary president loaned me ten thousand dollars, and I went to
a close friend with an accounting and real estate background and proposed that we form a partnership and develop. He agreed, and we began
by building a rental community in St. Petersburg.

We then developed an office building in downtown St. Petersburg,
which was built and leased. So far, so good. Our next venture was in
urban Tampa, my home, which was where I really wanted to be. The
search for that project resulted in a sophisticated urban infill development, over which I had operational control. Design was not my partner's
forte, nor was it that of our investor (a wealthy person whose land we
were developing).

So it was really my project: a seven-home private enclave, replete
with a brick street, a large fountain, special lighting and street furniture,
expensive landscaping, and an elegant entry wall and identification
signage. The homes were planned to sell in the $250,000 range, which
was, on a per square foot basis, on the high end for Tampa. We named
the project Audubon Park, after Audubon Place, the old and elegant enclave in New Orleans.

My partners had faith in my sense of design and encouraged me,
knowing of my anthropological background, to conduct the required
market research on which we would base our design. Using key informant interviewing techniques, I identified and interviewed about fifteen
South Tampa homeowners who lived in expensive homes. We talked
about what my homes should look and feel like, the amenities that

should be included, and the physical configurations of kitchens, family rooms, bedrooms, bathrooms, living rooms, and terraces that would be most appealing.

The consensus seemed to be that the homes should feel traditional; they should have hardwood floors, European kitchens, fireplaces, French doors, and terraces. Our price range was high, but the quality we would put in both the homes and the site would justify the price.

I selected our architects. They were friends, and people whose talent and dedication to design quality I admired. Based on my research and the cost parameters my partner and I established, the architects presented conceptual designs for seven homes, the first two of which would be constructed speculatively. The design and construction process for the property and the first two homes took about fifteen months, and I enjoyed almost every minute. The development was elegant, as were the first two homes. The project was published in two architectural journals and won several design awards. But the homes didn't sell quickly.

I had misinterpreted my market research. My informants told me to build homes with traditional elements, with amenities that would appeal to home buyers in that price range. What I had actually designed and built were homes of the then-new School of Post Modernism, an architectural style that *combines* traditional elements of architecture into a somewhat bolder, more shocking recombination. The critics loved the homes, but upwardly mobile, aesthetically insecure buyers—my buyers!—were scared away from homes their friends might not like.

Our investor partner opted out. We were forced to discount the house prices and sell the remaining lots to another builder, effectively ending that phase of my career.

While wondering what my next trick would be, I was contacted by architect friends who admired what we had done at Audubon Park. Three Tampa-area architectural firms had decided to merge, despite competing as rivals for years, in order to form a large (150 professionals and staff) architectural/planning firm that could compete with the large firms coming into Florida from other states.

Was I interested in becoming the new firm's planning director? Was I comfortable working with architects—lots of them? Could I manage? Was I conversant with the challenges of the consulting business? I answered yes, although it would all be a new experience. I knew that it would come to me; after all, I was an anthropologist.

I was hired, and spent the next several years learning the business of facilitating the work of architects (who often have trouble communicating verbally or understanding client needs) and providing urban planning services on a consulting basis.

I enjoyed the experience, but the company never found its way and painfully broke up into its original constituent members, for the most ironic and fundamental reason. The senior members of the three original firms, who believed they could merge their design and business philosophies, found they couldn't. It was a waste of time and money, and an expensive lesson for everyone involved. I was asked by each group to stay, and chose the new firm with the strongest design reputation. I became a partner in the firm, and then found during the next eighteen months that their specialties—secondary school and university buildings, and occasional projects like country clubs, churches, and museums—did not really require the services of a senior urban planner.

I was comfortably in a firm without quite enough to do. As an eternal junior partner, I didn't have enough influence in a firm of very strong senior architect partners. I concluded that I needed a graceful way to move on, and waited for an opportunity.

During the same period, the University of South Florida had begun a master of arts degree program in architecture, in conjunction with Florida A&M University in Tallahassee. The program had been long sought by the local architectural community and was accompanied by the formation of an urban design public service institute with a substantial operating budget and a nationally renowned urban designer recruited in as director.

As I was musing about my life's next chapter, the director lost his associate director, and I was approached about filling that role on an interim basis for one year, with the understanding that if I performed well, the position could probably be permanent. The position carried with it an associate professor rank in the School of Architecture and teaching responsibilities.

Over the past five years, I had become involved in the politics of the community, particularly with regard to planning and redevelopment issues, and had been appointed a member of the Hillsborough County Planning Commission, the organization where I began my career twelve years earlier.

The university position looked exciting and included the opportunity to become more professionally involved in the affairs of the community, and to do so as both a facilitator and an educator. I took the job, and my partners purchased my stock.

It was a very stimulating and difficult year. I soon realized that I had basic philosophical disagreements with the director regarding marketing and management issues and organizational philosophy. I did enjoy participating at the architecture school, however, and quickly learned the challenges of becoming a decent instructor.

The year allowed me to pursue community interests and gave me useful experience in the mysteries of organizational administration. As it drew to a close, I informed the director that I would not be applying for the permanent position and began preparing for the future.

What next? I regretted having to leave the university, and often wonder if I made the right decision, but it had really turned on my determination to avoid spending an extended period working for someone I just did not agree with on such a wide variety of issues.

The one variety of local planning I had not tried was my own practice. Several clients with whom I had enjoyed long relationships offered me the opportunity to represent them on an ongoing basis, which was an adequate enough income base to take the risk of going on my own.

One of the opportunities was to become the Executive Director, on a consulting basis, of the Ybor Channel Redevelopment Association, a private association of property owners on the eastern side of Tampa's downtown peninsula. The position allowed me to represent an entire area, positioning it for redevelopment through the planning and political processes in Tampa.

For six years I have had my own practice and spent my own time on the Planning Commission and other boards and organizations. The realities of cash flow, finding work, doing it, and collecting the income is a vivid lesson in entrepreneurship, one from which everyone would benefit. Nevertheless, I have found great satisfaction in the freedom of my own practice. I have no partners or employees.

Practicing alone has not limited me professionally; I am involved in the community in ways I see fit. My practice has expanded into areas that require more political strategy and positioning of issues than does traditional land use planning.

I am able to respond to new niches and opportunities more quickly than I could with a larger firm. Most recently, I have become very active in the area of urban planning research and testimony, as an expert witness in the growing field of eminent domain law, a market place that exists as a result of Florida's dramatic growth rate, progressive planning legislation, and eminent domain laws favorable to property owners.

I still teach a cultural anthropology course at the architecture school; I focus on ethnographic methods. It is simple stuff to anthropologists, but the principles are valid and powerful. Student architects, unlike many of the giants they admire, are willing to grapple with the fundamental necessity to understand their clients' needs and to discover the broad range of values, behaviors, and needs inherent in the future inhabitants of their designs. They will, I hope, learn to use ideas such as ethnographic research techniques and post-occupancy evaluation in the design of buildings, neighborhoods, and cities.

My role as member and three-time chair of the Planning Commission over the past eight years would not have been as productive without anthropological training. My earlier experience as a graduate student/ planner gave me insight, as an insider, into the organization's history and mission. I came on the commission with an understanding of both the historical urban planning process in the community and of the role of the Planning Commission over a significant period of time, as the legally mandated planning agency for the community, and as an institutional icon that was often the one voice of reason in a frenzy of growth-related economic development.

In 1985, Florida's legislature became concerned about the state's future and decided to make comprehensive planning a legal mandate. As a result, my two terms on the commission coincided with a new day for the influence of urban planning in my community; I was determined to make the most of it.

Applied anthropology has been useful for me in many ways as a planning commissioner. I make my living as an urban planning consultant, am involved in the politics of the community, and represent a number of clients with property interests affected by the Planning Commission's actions. All these factors made my appointment sensitive in terms of potential conflicts of interest. That sensitivity shaped my decision to alter my practice so as to avoid not only actual conflicts (such as appearing before the commission representing clients and lobbying staff on planning recommendations) but also perceived conflicts (appearing before area-elected officials on private planning matters).

The commission's Executive Director was hired from out of state the same month that I was appointed. I soon became his key informant and was able to significantly shorten his learning curve about the inner workings of our political, business, and ethnic communities. In return for my insider's knowledge, I gained his trust, and for eight years have had my counsel and insights well received by him.

My experience as a staff member years ago, while studying applied anthropology, helps me to understand the inner workings of the staff without meddling in their affairs, have empathy for their world view, and read the often subtle implications of their recommendations. It is fascinating to observe the constant and dynamic interplay of competing interests in the urban planning process, which is truly a metaphor for the life of a community and a model for observing the evolution of cultural values and social change in Florida.

Perhaps the most important aspect of my experience has been the realization that my anthropological orientation has helped me guide the commission's political course to avoid unnecessary pitfalls, traps, and mistakes. No matter what we do, which usually involves suggesting a better way to do something to the Mayor or the County Administrator, or telling a property owner or developer that his idea for developing his property isn't appropriate, we upset someone. Anthropology helps me recognize dangerous challenges and attacks before they happen, and the effective solution to the problem, by sensitizing me to other world views and other agendas.

My professional experiences, particularly as a member of the Planning Commission, have all been enhanced by my training. Ethnographic methods, the combination of insider and outsider perspectives on behavior, the use of network analysis and key informants, a sense of holism, and the reality of cultural relativity are basic concepts to anthropologists and invaluable to anyone involved in public policy making. I hope that the study of anthropology leads more applied anthropologists to positions in which the opportunity to help shape public policy is possible, for it is at that level of activity that ideas can often be shaped into long-term culture change and the tools of our discipline used to communicate ideas broadly.

Praying with Creationists

Christopher P. Toumey

Anthropologists have peculiar social needs. We expect little appreciation from our next-door neighbors, but we desperately need to be liked by the far-away peoples we study. We isolate ourselves from our neighbors by putting a wall of unique intellectual habits around ourselves, but then the opposite holds true when we travel far away.

Winning the respect of the ones we study is desperately important to us. The friendships we form with far-away peoples give us great confidence that the occupation of seeing into strangers' lives goes well.

Another reason why we court their acceptance is a simple matter of professional vanity. Our colorful tales of succeeding among exotic peoples are a precious currency that buys status in our profession. One-upmanship to an anthropologist means that the people you study have congratulated you for having penetrated their culture, so that later you can repeat their praise to your fellow anthropologists.

My favorite example of this process comes from Napoleon Chagnon's book on the Yanomamo, wherein the author tells us how these people thrive in a web of sexual mischief, casual violence, and daily drug use. Through most of his book he stands apart as an objective observer, understandably uninvolved in the more brutal moments of Yanomamo life.

The reader may well wonder how he could stay so detached. But then, near the end, he tells of the time he, too, took the drug *ebene*. He, too, colors himself with their body paint and chants their shaman songs. He, too, has the holy hallucinations of tiny spirits dancing to his orders. This, of course, turns out to be the day he is accepted as a man by the Yanomamo men, and he passes easily between the two worlds of the North American scientist and the South American Indian.

This kind of accomplishment is a common motif in our writing, especially among the brand-new Ph.D.'s displaying their achievements for the first time. The books and journals of our profession are replete with such vignettes: "The day I was accepted as a human by the Heebie-Jeebies," or "How I became a man among the Mumbo-Jumbo."

I, too, have danced my way through the apprentice's rituals of this peculiar profession, carefully executing the steps that led to a Ph.D. I, too, appreciate the approval of the folks I studied. And, yes, I, too, try to convert that approval into status among my peers.

"My tribe," the ones I studied for my dissertation, were the "scientific creationists," that is, fundamentalist Christians who dedicate themselves to defacing all the first principles of anthropology, including humanism and cultural relativism, but especially evolutionary thought. To get to the people who were actively involved in advocating creationism, I contacted those who wrote letters to the editor in favor of creationism in the state's newspapers. Almost every one of them agreed to be interviewed. Through these contacts, I met several members of a local creationist study group. We discussed what I was doing, and when I asked for their membership list, they kindly gave me a copy. With it I contacted more people to interview. Some of my interviewees suggested other creationists for me to interview. From among the letter writers, the members of the study group, and the secondary references, I interviewed dozens of individuals who were creationist activists.

I did everything I honestly could to make my feelings and intentions clear. I told them that I was not a creationist, and that I disagreed with much of what they believed; however, I continued, it distressed me to see that creationists were sorely misunderstood by journalists and evolutionists. I said that I wanted to overcome the cardboard caricatures of creationists (e.g., that creationism today was merely a reprise of the Scopes Trial of 1925).

After word got around about what I was doing, it was concluded that I was harmless, and the local creationist study group invited me to come to its meetings. These were held about ten times a year, on the second Thursday of the month. Usually a small group of men gathered at the comfortable suburban home of a science professor from one of the local universities, where they would begin the meeting with a prayer, then spend the evening in a serious study of scientific topics that reflected on creationism, and finally end with another prayer.

On most evenings the group consisted of the same familiar people. In addition to the host, they were: another science professor at the same university; a computer engineer from IBM; an electronics technician; a laboratory scientist from a major pharmaceutical firm, and another from a federal government research facility; and two medical doctors. Others who attended occasionally were college students, electrical engineers, and more laboratory scientists.

I, too, had a role of sorts. If I could have, I would have hid behind my notebook and my Bible, for all I wanted was a fly-on-the-wall view of the creationist group. But that was impossible because these were small, friendly meetings at which the members of the group made me feel welcome, often asking for my professional opinions and personal feelings about creationism. I participated modestly by contributing my knowledge of the history of evolutionary and anti-evolutionary thought, which they liked to hear about. I became by default the group's unofficial historian of creationism. This was a strange thing for me, an evolutionist explaining the history of creationism to a group of creationists, but I was happy to make myself useful, and they appreciated my esoteric expertise.

Another role I acquired was that of being a source for contacts. Creationism was very much in the news in North Carolina at that time, and I was the one person in the state who was working on the topic full-time. I often found myself passing on names and phone numbers of creationists to other creationists, of evolutionists to evolutionists, even of putting creationists and evolutionists in contact with each other.

I also found that evolutionists frequently asked for my advice on combating creationism. While I agreed with their philosophy, I could hardly use personal information about creationists, gathered in confidential interviews, against my interviewees. Thus my habit was to speak in general terms about information and opinion that was more or less common knowledge. I drew a line between that sort of information and other information that might betray the trust of the creationists I was interviewing. When in doubt, I cautiously protected the latter kind of information.

After I finished my fieldwork, the potential for conflict of interest came very close to me. I was involved, along with about twenty-five other academics, in an effort to dissuade a local North Carolina school board from instituting creationism in a public school science curriculum. My contribution did not betray the confidentiality of any of my creationist contacts, since I carefully avoided using personal information, either from my interviews or from my participant-observation work. Nevertheless, I realized that future activities of this sort could make my personal knowledge very relevant, even though it was off-limits. In addition, I understood that even if I never betrayed anyone's confidentiality, the creationists of North Carolina might *suspect* that I was doing so anyway, which would be almost as bad as a genuine ethical conflict of interest.

After worrying a great deal, I found an effective solution to my ethical dilemma. I moved to Kentucky. This was not the reason why I moved to Kentucky; I had very good reasons, unrelated to creationism, for going there. But I must admit I appreciated getting away from the potential for conflict of interest.

Anyway, while I was doing my fieldwork, I figured that "my tribe," my middle-class American white Anglo-Saxon Protestant tribe, was not the kind to initiate me as a man among their men. Toumey among the creationists was not going to end up like Chagnon among the Yanomamo. But there was lots to do, anyway, and lots to learn, especially on those once-a-month Thursdays when the local creationists assembled.

The main business of the meeting one night was a creationist film about hominid fossils. Its narrator discussed Piltdown Man to make the point that evolutionary assumptions lead to foolish mistakes. He also showed the dental arcades of a young girl and a chimpanzee to suggest that it was easy to overemphasize superficial similarities, after which he stressed human-chimp differences. Then he interviewed a British paleontologist who spoke of the difficulties of forensic reconstruction, with the film implying that it was unreliable. The movie concluded with the idea that anatomical similarities between species should be interpreted as functional similarities designed by God, not as phyletic links from common ancestry shared by humans and apes.

Immediately after the film, the leader of the group turned to me, saying, "Chris, you're an anthropologist. You probably know these fossils better than we do. Maybe you can tell us what weaknesses the film had that we didn't notice because we're creationists." I thought for a moment and replied that this film, like much creationist literature, described differences between hominid fossils in terms of two extreme polarities, labeling them either as obvious apes or as modern humans, with nothing transitional in between. I went on to point out that there is a credible continuum of fossil features between the apelike early australopithecines and the more recent Cro-Magnons. I gave the example of KNM-ER 1470, the East African skull dated at a little under two million years, which I said was a mix of australopithecine and human features, representing a transition between late australopithecines and early humans. This fossil, I told them, could not be dismissed by labeling it either as pure ape or pure human; I said as tactfully as I could that the creationists should not overlook this.

One of the creationists responded that he'd heard that Neanderthal skulls fit within the range of modern human variation. Another man commented that, if Neanderthals were within the modern human range, as creationists say, then creationist scientists ought to be able to find some Neanderthals in the world's population today. He was right, and none of us knew what to say to that.

At this point it was obviously time to end the meeting. The creationists and I looked at the man who usually said the closing prayer. This time, however, the leader did not turn to him. He turned to me. "Chris," he said, "will you lead us in our closing prayer?"

This request stunned me. I thought to say, no, I'm the anthropologist, the observer, the evolutionist, the guy you don't really want to lead you in prayer. But I also saw that the leader was honoring me by asking me. He was telling me that he appreciated my honesty about fossils. And the leader's invitation meant that he and the group trusted me enough to grant me their greatest honor, that is, the spiritual responsibility of leading them in prayer. This tribute I could not decline.

First I stifled my instinct to blurt out a Hail Mary—not the kind of prayer he invited me to lead. In my mind I quickly rushed through the pattern of an evangelical prayer, of which I had heard hundreds during my fieldwork. First, the one praying invokes the person of God the Father, saying "Heavenly Father" or "Our Father in heaven" or something along those lines. Second, it is necessary to say that the people praying are gathered in His name, or in His presence, or in His grace. Third, the one leading the prayer states the purpose or theme of the occasion: "to share fellowship with so-and-so," for example, or "to renew our faith." This part can include any topic or comment relevant to the occasion. It is also the place to tell God what's on your mind, knowing that other people are listening carefully to hear it. Finally, there is mention of Jesus Christ; the most common convention is to say, "We pray this in Jesus' name."

I took a breath and started in a calm, clear voice. "God our Father, as we gather here tonight in your heavenly presence, we're real glad to be able to come together again to study the wonders of your creation, and to share fellowship with each other for this purpose. We're happy that these folks have been able to be here tonight. We don't always understand what you mean in the creation you've given us, and we don't always agree about it. But we're thankful for this wonderful gift you've given us. We say this in Jesus' name."

My prayer drew no comment, so I must have done it right. I wasn't much of a conversationalist as we moved to the kitchen for coffee and donuts, because I was still thrilled that I had been asked to lead the closing prayer. Usually when something goes to my head like that, I shut my mouth so I don't say something stupid. Of course, prayer is supposed to make you pious, not puffed up with pride, but I couldn't help it. I had been honored, and I felt great.

While driving home that night, it came to me that my moment of praying with creationists was more than a matter of creationism. It was also the anthropologist's epiphany that I had thought would never happen to me. I couldn't help thinking that while I stayed in North Carolina to study creationists, most of my fellow graduate students headed for places like Trinidad or Nepal or Tonga. I loved those men and women and I missed them. And I regretted that when they had their necessary episodes of being accepted as a real man or a true woman by "their tribes" in those lands, I would have nothing more special than the mundane days of a middle-class American intellectual taking notes on other middle-class Americans, mostly within the borders of the state of North Carolina. I figured that if the precious epiphany that marks an anthropologist was going to elude anyone, I was the one it was going to elude.

But, by golly, it had touched me, and it had done so right in the bosom of bourgeois U.S.A. True, this required no illicit drugs like *ebene*. It only needed the simple words that said, "Chris, will you lead us in our closing prayer?" That was fine with me, because I had had one of those magic instances, a little window in human time when I was myself, the anthropologist observing, and a creationist worshiping, both at the same time. The double sensation had filled even me, for my tribe had pronounced me to be a man among men, on their terms.

After I got over that sensation, I had one last bit of business to consider, which was the ethics of my experience. I did not want to deceive my creationist friends about my work or my beliefs. Again and again, I had told them that I was not a creationist and was not trying to pose as one.

On the other hand, I seldom volunteered my own views. Since the members of the study group saw me at most of the meetings, and since I did not argue against creationism, they might have thought I was with them in their creationist beliefs.

I tried to keep my behavior somewhere in a middle course: not so private that my stance was concealed, but not so formal that my status was irksome. With this issue on my mind, I feared that saying the prayer would tilt things too much toward the mistaken belief that I was becoming a creationist.

A month later I figured out that my fears had been quite groundless, and that the creationists were not nearly as fickle as I feared. After the evening of my evangelical prayer, they took to introducing me to other creationists by saying, "This is Chris Toumey. He's an evolutionist, but he's our friend."

This essay is adapted from *God's Own Scientists,* by Christopher P. Toumey (Rutgers University Press, 1994). A longer version originally appeared in *Soundings* (76[1]:59–84) in 1993.

The Development of an Undergraduate Applied Anthropology Training Program

Susan Emley Keefe

Applied anthropology is most often described as a discipline for professional practicing anthropologists who have had graduate training. Very little attention has been paid to the impact applied anthropology can have on students at the undergraduate level. In a study carried out in 1988, only ten formal applied anthropology undergraduate programs were identified at American universities that do not have a graduate program in anthropology (Keefe 1988). In the Department of Anthropology at Appalachian State University (which has no graduate-level program), we have always put an emphasis on undergraduates. Beginning fifteen years ago, we determined that applied anthropology was one of the strengths of our faculty and was something that should be valuable to our majors, most of whom do not go on to graduate school in anthropology but who could have careers employing the anthropological perspective. In the development of our undergraduate applied anthropology program, we have come to appreciate its value for students providing both training in anthropological practitioners' method and theory *and* career directions following graduation.

In this essay, I describe the organization and content of the undergraduate applied anthropology program at Appalachian State University. The program consists of three formal/informal degree tracks focused on applied anthropology, archeology, and physical/forensic anthropology. There are also two applied programs affiliated with the department that provide opportunities for undergraduates but also serve broader purposes: the Sustainable Development Program and the Laboratories of Archeological Science (ASULAS). These will be briefly described insofar as they relate to the undergraduate applied anthropology program.

THE APPLIED ANTHROPOLOGY CONCENTRATION

Our department offers three bachelor of arts degrees: the General Anthropology degree, the Applied Concentration, and the Archeology Concentration. Each of these requires a core of six courses so that the student
is introduced to cultural anthropology, physical anthropology, and archeology at the lower division level, and methodology, anthropological
theory, and a senior seminar at the upper division level. The Applied
Concentration requires, in addition, the course "Applied Anthropology"
and an internship. Other course work related to the student's career focus
may be suggested as electives within or outside of the major. A student interested in medical anthropology, for example, might be advised
to take courses such as "Medical Anthropology," "Medical Sociology,"
"Principles of Epidemiology," "Consumer Health Education," or "Nutrition and Health" (the last four being offered in other departments on
campus). Most students in the Applied Concentration are interested in
cultural anthropology, although archeology and physical anthropology
interests can be accommodated through the electives.

There has been a sharp increase in the number of students opting
for the Applied Concentration in the last five years; 26 percent of our
majors are currently enrolled in this degree program. This figure reflects national trends indicating an upswing in general student interest
in the anthropology major as well as local campus trends indicating anthropology at A.S.U. more than doubled its number of majors between
1990 and 1995. With 126 anthropology majors, we have more majors
and award more undergraduate degrees in anthropology than any other
institution in the state of North Carolina (public or private), with the ex-
ception of the University of North Carolina at Chapel Hill. The increase
in Applied Concentration majors also reflects the impact of the Sustainable Development Program, an interdisciplinary program that was
created in 1991 and is housed administratively in our department (primarily because the director, Dr. Jeff Boyer, is an anthropologist). Many
of our majors take a minor in Sustainable Development, seeing an in-
terrelationship between the two programs. A popular interdisciplinary
minor (also established in 1991), Sustainable Development currently
serves approximately seventy-five students. Many of those nonanthropology majors attracted to the Sustainable Development minor, in turn,
have ultimately decided to declare an anthropology major.

The Applied Concentration turns students' attention to the application of anthropology beyond the classroom walls. This process begins with the required course I teach, "Applied Anthropology," which involves classroom work the first half of the semester and a mini-internship the second half of the semester. One of the required texts is *Anthropological Praxis* (Wulff and Fiske 1988). In this anthology of applied anthropology case studies, the editors have asked each of the authors to comment on the "anthropological difference" with regard to their specific project. In carrying out the mini-internship, students are also asked to reflect on the "anthropological difference" they made during the internship.

Setting up internships for an entire class is not easy, and a brief description of this process might be helpful. To begin with, the class size is limited to fifteen students in order to accommodate placement and supervision tasks. The process of internship placement begins the very first week of class. Local internship possibilities are described, with special emphasis on those that have worked well for students in the past. Students in this class have been placed in all kinds of internships in the vicinity of Boone, such as the Appalachian Cultural Center, the Town of Boone (Planning Department; Water Works Department), High Country Host (a tourism center), the Small Business Technical Development Center, the Blue Ridge Environmental Defense League, the Watauga County Sheriff's Department, Watauga Opportunities (a day program for the mentally handicapped), and the Western Watauga Community Center (serving the most rural end of the county).

After hearing the internship descriptions, each student is asked to indicate one or two appealing placement possibilities. Students must also indicate their time schedules and access to transportation, since internships may have specific requirements for time-of-day or travel. The instructor makes the first contact with the agency and secures permission for the student to interview for the internship. If the agency has not had an anthropology intern before, this is also the time to describe the goals and requirements of the internship to the prospective field supervisor and to encourage feedback on the student's work. Students are then given the name, address, and telephone number of their field supervisor and are asked to call for an appointment. Each student must personally visit the field supervisor to discuss the potential internship and to obtain a written contract regarding internship requirements to be signed by all parties (student, field supervisor, and faculty supervisor). The internship contract is due the fifth week of the semester, assuring an easy transition to the internship in the second half of the semester.

Students come together twice as a class during the mini-internships to share experiences and problems. (The first of these meetings is in the second week of the internship so that problems can be ironed out as soon as possible.) Otherwise, the assignment is to serve eight hours per week at the agency, maintain contact with the instructor, and keep a journal as a written record of the experience. Guidelines for the journal ask the student to make observations regarding: (1) the daily tasks undertaken during the internship; (2) personal reactions and individual reflection concerning the internship experience (especially as a potential career field); (3) ethnographic observations about the agency, employees, clients, and the intern's relationship to the setting; and (4) insight into the "anthropological difference" made by the intern. This fourth task is always the most difficult part of the assignment but it is potentially the most valuable. The instructor also makes a site visit to each agency while the intern is present and asks the field supervisors to turn in written evaluations of interns at the end of the semester.

The mini-internship is inevitably the most memorable part of the "Applied Anthropology" course for students. Coming together and sharing internship experiences as a class serves to further expose students to other internship and career options. In many cases, the experience leads to a formal internship or a part-time job.

The other required course for the applied concentration is the formal internship. Formal internships are offered any time of the year, but the majority are arranged during the summer. Summer internships give the student the most intense experience as they are required to work full-time in an agency. An internship may be arranged for a student in any anthropology degree program. Demand for internships has certainly grown with the increase in students majoring in the Applied Concentration. Demand, however, extends beyond this degree program: fully one-third of our students in the past sixteen years have enrolled in an internship prior to graduation. The success of our internship program can be attributed to many things: faculty development of worthwhile internship placements; positive student evaluation of internships; and the generally recognized relationship between internships and informed career choices following graduation. A recent survey by Northwestern

University, for example, found that 58 percent of students who worked as interns received permanent job offers at graduation compared to only 30 percent of all graduates finishing college.

Internships require a departmental application process and approval by a faculty committee, as a means of ensuring quality control over the curriculum. Once approved, a written contract signed by the student, field supervisor, and faculty supervisor is required. Internship placements have been varied and are generally arranged to suit the individual needs and interests of students. Students have been placed in some forty agencies since 1978. Only about one-third of these are local agencies. In fact, almost half of the agencies are located outside North Carolina, including six international internships. We have a number of standing internships in the American Southwest, including Chaco Culture National Historical Park, Hubble Trading Post National Historic Site, and the Bureau of Land Management. The faculty member who developed these southwestern internships, Dr. Harvard Ayers, leads a field trip to the Southwest each spring break that feeds students into these placements.

Preparation for the internship generally involves related course work, which may include recommended courses and independent studies; requirements in other courses (such as research papers) may be arranged so they focus on an internship-related topic. Internship requirements include: (1) a fixed number of internship hours at the agency based on credit hours sought (e.g., a three-hour internship requires 160 agency hours; a six-hour internship requires 320 agency hours); (2) frequent contact with the faculty supervisor; (3) an evaluation by the field supervisor; and (4) a written journal documenting the experience. There should be a site visit by the faculty supervisor (although this may not be possible in the case of distant placements).

In the Applied Concentration, students have two internship experiences by the time they graduate (in "Applied Anthropology" and in the formal internship). Oftentimes, the internship experiences are critical in charting the course students will take upon graduation. As an example, one student in the "Applied Anthropology" course wanted to work with people of other cultures. The town of Boone does not have many multicultural venues, so the student was encouraged to work with international students on campus in the tutoring project of the Learning Assistance Program. Two years later, she decided to apply to the M.A. Program in English as a Second Language at U.N.C.-Charlotte. As another example, a student interested in museum work took several museum studies courses in the history department, volunteered in the Appalachian Cultural Museum on campus, interned with the Cultural Museum as part of the "Applied Anthropology" course, and ultimately had a formal internship with that museum. After graduation, he was hired as the Appalachian Cultural Museum's Community Education Director.

THE ARCHEOLOGY CONCENTRATION

The Bachelor of Arts degree in Anthropology with an Archeology Concentration was established in 1993 to prescribe course work for students interested in going on in archeology after graduation either in contract archeology work or in graduate studies. Twenty percent of our majors are currently enrolled in this degree program. In addition to the core courses required of all majors, those in the Archeology Concentration must take an archeology laboratory course, an archeological area studies course, the course "Archeological Method and Theory," and the archeology field school. Majors in this concentration are also strongly encouraged to minor in a physical or biological science.

The archeology field school is taught each summer and is a prerequisite for certain courses, such as archeological internships and the course "Archeological Site Reports." Archeology instructors alternate teaching the field school, and the instructor teaching the field school in the summer also teaches "Archeology Laboratory Methods" in the fall, generally analyzing materials collected during the summer field school. Students can take a sequence of courses collecting archeological material in the field school, analyzing those materials in the laboratory, and, finally, producing a site report based on the archeological materials.

There are numerous opportunities available for students to participate in supervised archeological fieldwork as members of various archeology classes, as volunteers on archeology projects, and as paid employees on archeological contracts. The department's Public Archeology Program, established in 1988 by Dr. Tom Whyte, incorporates members of the public as well as students in archeological projects. Sometimes this arrangement is required by funding agencies as part of cost-share agreements in the way of volunteer labor. Alumni and students are also included as employees on archeological contract work by ASULAS throughout the year.

Internships are sometimes arranged for students in the Archeology Concentration, adding to their experience in the field. Standing internships at Chaco Culture National Historical Park, for example, are suited for archeology students. Chaco Canyon, New Mexico, has some of the best preserved archeological sites in the country, and student interns assist park rangers in the Visitor Center and as guides in the canyon. Sometimes they are assigned as research assistants to archeologists working in the park. Internships have also been arranged in the southeastern United States with the U.S. Forest Service and with ASULAS. As an example of the progression of experiences, one student did an archeological internship with the Bureau of Land Management in southeastern Utah and later was admitted to graduate school at Eastern New Mexico University. He is currently enrolled in the Ph.D. program at the University of New Mexico.

PHYSICAL/FORENSIC ANTHROPOLOGY

Although we have no formal degree concentration in physical/forensic anthropology, there is a cohort of students with this interest who are served through advisement regarding a course of study. Course work offered by Dr. Harvard Ayers in the department includes "Physical Anthropology," "Forensic Anthropology," and "Human Osteology." Related course work offered elsewhere in the university includes "Human Anatomy and Physiology," "Kinesiology," "Introduction to Zoology," and "Comparative Vertebrate Zoology." Students with this interest often opt for the bachelor of science degree, which requires the same anthropology core courses listed earlier, fewer anthropology electives, and a multidisciplinary concentration that can incorporate the related course work just mentioned. These students are also strongly encouraged to obtain a good background in the natural sciences, particularly biology.

In the physical/forensic courses offered in anthropology, students are introduced to opportunities for research and internships through field trips to the Forensic Laboratory at the University of Tennessee in Knoxville, and to the Smithsonian Institution, among others. Internships have been arranged for students at the North Carolina Medical Examiner's Office and the Smithsonian Museum of Natural History. In one case, a student interned at the North Carolina Medical Examiner's Office and then, after graduation, went to Mortician's School. He is currently applying to graduate school in forensic anthropology.

ANCILLARY APPLIED PROGRAMS: SUSTAINABLE DEVELOPMENT AND LABORATORIES OF ARCHEOLOGICAL SCIENCE

There are two programs administered within the department that contribute in important ways to the undergraduate applied anthropology program: the Sustainable Development Program and the Laboratories of Archeological Science. Similar programs have been cited by the American Anthropological Association as useful for strengthening departments of anthropology over the next twenty-five years (Givens 1994a, 1994b).

Sustainable development, as defined at Appalachian State University, "is a process of meeting basic human needs through socio-economic activity that does not undermine the culture of a people or the environments in which they live. Through an integrated set of social, cultural, environmental, scientific, technical, economic, and political considerations, sustainable development advocates seek to develop and disseminate improvements that can promote a more livable 21st century for humans and life in all its diversity" (Sustainable Development Program 1991).

The Sustainable Development Program administers both an interdisciplinary academic curriculum and a program of applied research and service. The curriculum is focused at present on the undergraduate minor. A graduate-level concentration has also been approved, and plans are moving forward to approve a graduate minor.

The Sustainable Development Program has sponsored several international efforts on behalf of sustainable research and development, extending to Costa Rica, Honduras, Poland, and Slovakia. In Honduras, the director has organized two work-study summer programs involving students. During the summer of 1995, students assisted medical professionals in the development of a peasant-led barefoot doctor program in rural Honduras.

Appalachian State University Laboratories for Archeological Sciences (ASULAS) was established in 1993 for the purpose of undertaking contract archeology as well as long-term research involving regional and international archeological projects. ASULAS has been extremely successful in funding archeological projects in the region, generating a budget in excess of one hundred thousand dollars (through contracts with T.V.A., the U.S. Forest Service, various state agencies, and private firms) and at least fifty-nine opportunities for student involvement in archeological investigations in the first year of operation. The director of ASULAS, Dr. Larry Kimball, is also pursuing coordination of research opportunities at a paleolithic site with an archeological team at Northern Ossetia University, North Ossetia (formerly part of the Soviet Union), which may ultimately involve student exchanges.

These departmentally affiliated programs provide additional support and opportunities for students in applied anthropology. We anticipate the undergraduate applied anthropology program will continue to grow as these ancillary programs are strengthened.

CONCLUSION

In conclusion, our program demonstrates the kind of applied undergraduate training program that can be developed given persistence and consistent direction. We are a relatively small department of nine faculty with modest resources at a regional comprehensive state university. Nevertheless, we have expanded in the past seven years in the directions of public archeology, sustainable development, and contract archeology, successfully adding a faculty member with each new program. Each of these programs accommodates student interest and public outreach. Furthermore, each program has brought public recognition and resources (via the news media and funding opportunities) to our department. Evaluations of interns and our program by agencies and field supervisors have been overwhelmingly positive. We would encourage other departments to develop applied anthropology programs at the undergraduate level. It is good for the students. It is good for departments of anthropology. And it is good for society.

REFERENCES

Givens, David B. 1994a. Sociocultural Anthropology—The Next 25 Years. *Anthropology Newsletter* 35(4):1.

————. 1994b. Archaeology—The Next 25 Years. *Anthropology Newsletter* 35(6):1 and 4.

Keefe, Susan Emley. 1988. Applied Anthropology for Undergraduates. In *Anthropology for Tomorrow: Creating Practitioner-oriented Applied Anthropology Programs,* ed. Robert T. Trotter II, pp. 22–30. Washington, DC: American Anthropological Association.

Sustainable Development Program. 1991. *Program Brochure.* Boone, NC: Appalachian State University.

Wulff, Robert M., and Shirley J. Fiske. 1988. *Anthropological Praxis: Translating Knowledge into Action.* Boulder, CO: Westview Press.

The Appalachia Tourism Project: Applied Anthropology in an Appalachian Coal Mining Town

Mary B. La Lone

This essay describes a mutually beneficial partnership that developed between an anthropologist and an Appalachian coal mining town urgently seeking economic survival through a grassroots community development project. As an anthropologist, I approached this relationship with two goals: 1) to assist the town's effort to develop ideas for heritage tourism; and 2) to use my consulting relationship as a vehicle through which students could learn from a participatory experience in an off-campus community. In this essay I examine the evolution of this applied anthropology project and measure its successes.

BACKGROUND AND SENSE OF PROBLEM

Like many towns in southwest Virginia, the Town of Appalachia was founded and flourished on the coal mining economy of its region, and it became economically dependent on mining as its principal source of employment and income. Today, that economic situation has radically and rapidly changed: the coal industry is no longer able to serve as the economic base for the town. During the past five or six years, the mines have been scaling down operations and laying off miners. Faced with the rapid decline of the coal mining industry, and seeing the parallel decline of the town's economy, the town is on an economic survival mission—it is desperately looking for alternative forms of economic development. In 1990, citizens of the Town of Appalachia decided it was time to take an active role in reshaping the future of the town and the region. A grass-roots development effort was born from within the community.

Although the town has considered the idea of attracting industry as a form of development, that possibility is limited since the town is not located on a major interstate highway and is situated in a valley too narrow to accommodate an industrial park. The citizens therefore concluded that the cultural heritage and natural beauty of the Appalachian mountains might facilitate development based on tourism. So the community has been exploring the ways in which tourism might generate income, as well as preserve and celebrate the coal mining heritage of which the Appalachian people are extremely proud.

STAGE 1: ANTHROPOLOGIST AND LANDSCAPE ARCHITECT JOIN FORCES, JANUARY–MAY 1992

For two years, the community movement grew and began searching for ways to get the project off the ground. The town turned to the Community Design Center at Virginia Polytechnic Institute for assistance, and at the beginning of 1992 Charlene Browne, a landscape architect at Virginia Tech, took on the assignment as a design project for her landscape architecture studio class. She invited me to join forces with her in a five-month landscape architecture project to develop a preliminary set of designs for tourism in Appalachia. Acting as an anthropological consultant to the town and class, I especially focused on incorporating into the design work the community-oriented approach of applied anthropology and an understanding of the region's cultural history. This first stage of the tourism project had a number of benefits for the town and the academics. Over the five-month period, the town became increasingly comfortable about working with professors and students, local interest in the tourism project sprang up and spread like wildfire, and in May the community enthusiastically examined the student designs in a well-attended town meeting. Our end product was a design report entitled *Echoes of the Past—Vitality for the Future* (Browne 1992; Browne and La Lone 1992), which presented the town with a set of preliminary architectural designs for tourism. Based on our *Echoes* report, the town applied for, and won, a $34,000 grant from the United States Forest Service to study the feasibility of developing tourism. We considered this first work successful but preliminary, and had intended to continue developing our joint effort. My colleague, however, left Virginia Tech and moved away from the region in the summer of 1992.

INTERIM EVENTS

Over the next year, I continued my relationship with the town, but primarily turned my interests to developing and conducting a second project, a historical anthropology research project focused on reconstructing the cultural history of the coal mining communities that once surrounded the Town of Appalachia. While not directly involved in the tourism project, I was building an active teaching partnership between myself and the town as I and my students collected oral histories for the historical project (La Lone 1994c, 1994d).

Meanwhile, the town had bid out its grant and contracted with a professional development team to do the feasibility study. I therefore sat back to watch what they would do. As it turned out, through my observations and conversations with the townspeople, I received an excellent education on how not to conduct a development project, and I came to appreciate even more how applied anthropology's community-oriented approach to development differs greatly from nonanthropological approaches. From an applied anthropology standpoint, the team's procedure for studying the town's needs and resources left much to be desired, since they had little contact with the town during the six-month contract period. Their first visit to the town, which I happened to observe, involved sending three people dressed in cosmopolitan-style clothing to conduct a whirlwind schedule of fifteen-minute interviews packed into a two-day period. Mind you, this is a small Appalachian town where the pace of life is slow, many residents have a distrust of city folk, and they expect people to get to know one another as part of a conversation. Where was the rapport-building and time needed to gain an ethnographic knowledge of the place, including the goals, needs, and human resources of the community? At the end of the two days, the consultants told the town tourism committee that most of its ideas were probably unworkable, then left the region not to be heard from again for nearly six months. The Town Clerk told me that after making two additional one-day visits, and asking for two extensions to file their report,

the consultants turned in a report that left many people in the town un-
happy with its content, confused, and frustrated about where its grant
money had gone.

STAGE 2: THE FALL 1993 ECONOMIC
ANTHROPOLOGY CLASS PROJECT

In the summer of 1993, the town and I found our interests converging.
The citizens were just dealing with their frustration over the grant fiasco
when news arrived that the region's principal mining company was
threatening to shut down its facilities much earlier than the town had expected. For my part, I was in the process of looking for a experiential
learning project to build into my "Economic Anthropology" class in the
upcoming semester. Each time I teach the class, I try to bring economics
to life for the students by involving them in participatory learning projects in their local surroundings (La Lone 1994b, 1994c, 1994d, 1994e,
1994f; Wagner and La Lone 1993). I realized that I could once again
assist the town's efforts to explore ideas for heritage tourism and, at the
same time, develop a class project that would provide my students with
an excellent learning opportunity to apply their economic anthropology
to a real case. With limited resources at its disposal, the town was quite
willing to work with the class and have the students participate in this
applied anthropology endeavor. So, the anthropologist and town re-
joined efforts in a mutually beneficial partnership for the fall 1993
semester.

For the "Economic Anthropology" class, I developed a semester-long
class project (fifteen weeks) designed to involve students directly in the
process of assessing and refining ideas for Appalachia's development
through tourism. The project was funded jointly by the Radford University Foundation and the Honors Program. I wanted my class to pick up
where the *Echoes* Stage 1 had left off in May 1992. Our *Echoes* report
was good, but it had been intended as a set of conceptual architectural
designs, not a researched exploration of the means of developing
tourism. As an anthropologist, I felt that a more substantive exploration
and discussion of heritage tourism was still needed, and this was the
task I set for Stage 2. Participants in the class were asked to work together as a cooperative research team. Their challenge was to assess the
town's ideas for tourism, research and reshape the ideas, and then to de-

velop a set of "working ideas" on how the town might develop a viable form of heritage tourism.

As professor and project director, I established a set of guidelines that defined how much the team should tackle and the particular approaches they should take (La Lone 1994a). The research team was specifically asked to examine ways in which the Town of Appalachia could put together a "sustainable tourism package" that integrated a number of themes important to the community. The students were asked to concentrate on doing their best to develop positive ways in which the town could further its expressed desire to explore tourism as a form of development. In addition to setting the guidelines/procedures for the study, I set up project phasing and due dates, gave related reading assignments, held class discussions on applied anthropology and the wider economic development theoretical issues reflected in this project, and led weekly brainstorming/planning sessions.

TRANSLATING THE GUIDELINES INTO RESEARCH AND RECOMMENDATIONS

One of the key guiding concepts that shaped the students' work was applied anthropology's "community-oriented" approach to development. The approach of an applied anthropologist to a development project is to work closely with the community and to plan for the community. This is very different from an approach that views the designer/planner as the "expert" who assesses and plans changes with limited input or participation from the community. From conversations while working with my landscape architect colleague (who also had training in anthropology), as well as observations of the grant team's procedure, I had been disturbed to discover that applied anthropology's community orientation is not necessarily shared by practitioners of other fields. So, the emphasis on this project was on developing an atmosphere of cooperative planning between the town and the students. After studying the *Echoes* report, and discussing its strengths and weaknesses, the students went to Appalachia for a cooperative discussion of ideas with the people involved in the community effort. Appalachia community members held a number of orientation sessions for the students, providing opportunities for them to learn firsthand of the community's reasons for wanting tourism, to learn of the concerns and feelings of this community toward the town's past and its future, and to learn about the efforts it had already undertaken—in other words, to orient the students to and for the community. During these conversations, the students were impressed by the energy and human resources of the townspeople, and they came to understand why the town was focusing on heritage tourism. Later, the students made return visits to the town to work out their ideas with community members, most especially Diane Reece, Bobby Dorton, Lewis Henegar, and Dewey Rowland. They discussed the feasibility of those ideas, and brainstormed new ones. They then used those community discussions to further shape their research directions and refine their ideas.

The emphasis on "planning for the community" also shaped the type of thinking I wanted the students to do. Since it was the town's expressed desire that we consider ideas for developing heritage tourism specifically, the students were asked to honor that request and to treat it seriously. There undoubtedly are negative aspects to tourism and some potential obstacles to tourism in this region; moreover, some developers might find reasons for writing off the town's desires as impossible from the very start. Nevertheless, our research team was asked to try to take on the challenge of exploring ways to solve or work around the negative aspects and barriers to tourism. In this case I did not feel that it was our place, nor was it a very productive approach, to take a dismissive attitude.

We spent a lot of our classroom time studying and weighing both negative and positive aspects of tourism. At first the students were surprised at my request that they help develop tourism for Appalachia since many of them had previously taken my "Culture Change and Survival" class in which they explored the negative impacts of tourism around the world. During the semester, we held weekly project discussions in which we addressed potential obstacles and conflicts and tried to brainstorm ways around them. In particular, we discussed the following problems and tried to incorporate ways to deal with these problems into our work.

1. Was tourism simply going to substitute one form of dependency for another? We held long discussions on the potential problems of outside investment and control, and the preponderance of low-wage jobs for the people of Appalachia. We recognized that such an outcome was probably inevitable, but community members were willing to take this risk since the loss of the coal mining industry was going to devastate the region. In our brainstorming sessions, we tried to think of ways that

employment and profit could stay within the region, for example by emphasizing the development of bed-and-breakfasts over chain hotel establishments.

2. How could we overcome the regional barriers to tourism, especially the region's remoteness and distance from interstate highways? Recognizing that remoteness was the greatest obstacle facing Appalachia, we focused much of our work on developing ideas for strong, targeted marketing and publicity campaigns to draw tourists into the region.

3. How could we overcome the potential negative impacts of tourism? One concern was how to avoid perpetuating the "dumb hillbilly" stereotype, and so our research focused on identifying and incorporating strong, positive Appalachian themes into our tourism planning: the coal mining and railroad heritage, the music and art traditions of Appalachian Mountain culture, and the natural beauty of this mountain region. A second concern was how to preserve the small-town community feeling valued by Appalachia's townspeople, while introducing tourism. We held long discussions on the differences in the types and scale of tourism, comparing the Cancun and Dollywood models to the Williamsburg model of heritage tourism as well as to smaller versions of living history heritage tourism, which we felt to be most appropriate for the Town of Appalachia.

4. How could tourism be a sustainable form of economic development? Sustainable tourism is a form of tourism that can support itself over time. We spent a great deal of time brainstorming ways to make tourism sustainable, including: a) looking for types of tourism activities that would not be entirely seasonal; b) thinking in terms of "phasing-in" activities over an extended period of time; c) considering ways of using some activities to generate publicity for other activities; and d) finding ways to join tourism development to other related nontourism forms of economic development whenever possible. With sustainability in mind, the team was directed to approach this project as the development of an integrated set of ideas that could work together, complementing one another, as a full "tourism package." The research team spent the semester discussing these issues, brainstorming ways to minimize the obstacles and capitalize on the strengths of the region, and researching ways to develop tourism. The class project goal was not to come up with a perfect plan for tourism in fifteen weeks—that was hardly possible. Instead, it was simply to come up with a set of "working ideas," ideas in

progress. As the final outcome of the semester's project, the team was asked to write up its research and recommendations in the form of a consulting report that the Town of Appalachia might use in its efforts to develop tourism, and the students enthusiastically agreed to take on this endeavor. The report entitled *Appalachia, Heart of the Appalachian Region: Working Ideas for Development* (La Lone, ed. 1994) presents the team's working ideas for developing a sustainable form of tourism in Appalachia.

A quick summary of the report demonstrates the scope of the project. In the first chapter, I discuss the parameters of the project and planning considerations for undertaking economic development through sustainable tourism. The following chapters were written by the students and explore ideas for developing a wide range of tourism activities. Heidi H. Field and Deanna Matthews examine ideas for revitalizing downtown Appalachia, emphasizing a culturally based design that integrates important themes in Appalachian Mountain culture and establishes the town as a festival center for mountain music and arts. Lin Usack explores ideas for developing heritage-based tourism around the region's coal mining history, including plans for developing a simulated coal mine and reconstructed coal mining camp that would operate as an interpretive or "living history" museum, and Alice T. Horn discusses ideas for railroad-based tourism involving the development of a working railroad tour, an annual festival, and a railroad museum. Wendy Detwiler and Astrid Haggerson examine ideas for developing a wide range of recreational activities to capitalize on the natural beauty and terrain of the mountain landscape, including the development of hiking, biking, and horseback riding trails, fishing and tubing activities, and camp grounds. Tackling some of the potential obstacles to tourism, Barbara Jones discusses ways to draw tourists into this semi-isolated region, emphasizing the need for all localities to pull together in a joint effort and the importance of combining tourism with other enterprises, such as bed-and-breakfasts and cottage industries, to create more sustainable forms of development. Sarah E. Merkle, Astrid Haggerson, and Lin Usack address the need for funding and marketing the tourism package by exploring ideas for raising funds, selecting target markets, creating advertising campaigns and other forms of promotion.

This 106-page consulting report represents an impressive body of work, especially when one realizes that it was written by undergraduate students. The students' report is equal in quality to the professional design team's report, to which the students did not have access while independently conducting their own study. The accomplishments of the students in this consulting report provide a clear demonstration of the value of incorporating applied anthropology projects into the classroom. The students were excited by the opportunity to apply their anthropology while participating in and contributing to an off-campus community. Their motivation was sustained throughout the semester as they worked to prepare a consulting report that was actually going to be presented to the town.

CONCLUSION

From the start, and throughout the past three years, there have been two overall goals to my applied anthropology relationship, or what I prefer to think of as a partnership with the Town of Appalachia. On one hand, I have been acting as a practicing anthropologist, and on the other hand, I have attempted to provide opportunities for students to learn through direct participation in applied anthropology.

Starting in early 1992, I ventured into my first experience doing applied anthropology by working as a consultant with the Town of Appalachia to further its efforts to explore the possibilities of developing heritage tourism. With the coal mining industry pulling out of a region economically dependent on coal, the town was clearly in need of assistance. I was initially attracted to the town's effort because of my interest in cultural survival and my concern that this Appalachian town faced a cultural survival threat due to the rapid demise of its economic base. Here was an opportunity for me to put into practice my anthropological knowledge of the potentials and limitations of culture change due to tourism. My goal was to help the town jump-start its tourism effort by advising and guiding it during the first stage of exploration, and then to undertake Stage 2 to provide a more in-depth exploration of tourism for the town's use. While my motivation to assist the town comes from a sense of advocacy, I take care that my actual consulting work tries to remain objective and that I advise on both the potentials and limitations of developing tourism.

At the same time, I recognized that my consulting relationship could be extended to provide students with excellent learning opportunities through direct experiential involvement in applied anthropology. On planning the "Economic Anthropology" class for fall 1993, I used my partnership with Appalachia to structure a full-semester opportunity for the students to gain hands-on involvement in applied anthropology. Not only was this an opportunity for students to apply their studies and to learn by doing, but it also gave them the opportunity to see the practical side of anthropology and to think about applied anthropology as a career possibility. I have never seen the level of motivation in a class equal the enthusiasm of this group of students, largely because of their excitement to be involved in a real applied anthropology project. This experience has taught me something very important: don't ever underestimate the abilities of undergraduate students to engage in very solid applied anthropological work. The class project was truly a mutually benefi-cial venture—the class was able to offer the town free consulting assis-tance to further develop its tourism ideas, and at the same time, the town provided a field site for participatory learning, where students could actually apply their studies and gain experience as practicing anthro-pologists.

The Town of Appalachia enthusiastically received the *Appalachia, Heart of the Appalachian Region* consulting report in February 1994. In fact, the Town Clerk told us that by April 1995 the town had already made extensive use of many of the ideas for town promotion and down-town revitalization contained in the report. In addition, it has used the consulting report as supporting documentation for multiple new grant applications submitted to Virginia state agencies in 1995, and has even sent a copy of the report to the governor's office. The town's effort to replace coal mining with heritage tourism takes on even greater urgency now that the region's principal coal mining company actually has begun the process of shutting down its operations (Gallagher 1995). I wish the Town of Appalachia much luck in pursuing its effort to develop an al-ternative economic base, and hope that the partnership forged between the town and anthropologist continues to make positive contributions to this effort.

REFERENCES

Browne, Charlene, ed. 1992. *Echoes of the Past—Vitality for the Future.* Blacksburg: Virginia Polytechnic Institute and State University, Landscape Architecture Program.

Browne, Charlene, and Mary B. La Lone. 1992. Historical Overview: The Land, the People, the Place, and the Design Program. In *Echoes of the Past— Vitality for the Future,* ed. Charlene Browne, pp. 1–19. Blacksburg: Virginia Polytechnic Institute and State University, Landscape Architecture Program.

Gallagher, F. J. 1995. 25 Mine Workers Laid Off: Westmoreland Selling Va. Plants. *Roanoke Times & World News* 21 June:B6.

La Lone, Mary B. 1994a. Appalachia, Heart of the Appalachian Region. In *Appalachia, Heart of the Appalachian Region: Working Ideas for Development,* ed. Mary La Lone, pp. 1–13. Radford, VA: Radford University, Honors Program and Department of Sociology and Anthropology.

———. 1994b. The Appalachia Tourism Project: Teaching through Participatory Involvement in Applied Anthropology. Paper presented at the annual meeting of the Society for Applied Anthropology, Cancun, Mexico.

———. 1994c. Extending the Classroom into the Community through Teaching Partnerships: The Development of a Teaching Partnership with an Appalachian Coal Mining Town. Paper presented at the annual meeting of the American Anthropological Association, Atlanta.

———. 1994d. The Place Named Appalachia: Preserving Its Past and Planning for Its Future. *ALCA-LINES* 3(1):4, 15.

———. 1994e. From Flea Markets to Appalachian Tourism: Enhancing Undergraduate Education in Anthropology with Experiential Learning Projects. *Connections* 5(1):1–4.

———. 1994f. The Flea Market: An Economic Anthropology Class Project. *Anthro Notes* 16(2):14–15.

La Lone, Mary B., ed. 1994. *Appalachia, Heart of the Appalachian Region: Working Ideas for Development.* Radford, VA: Radford University, Honors Program and Department of Sociology and Anthropology.

Wagner, Melinda Bollar, and Mary B. La Lone. 1993. Ethnography as a Teaching Tool: Immersing Students in the Local Culture. Paper presented at the annual meeting of the American Anthropological Association, Washington, DC.

Teaching Practitioners Practical Anthropology: A Course on the Rural South

V. Richard Persico Jr. and Roger G. Branch

Teaching students in a college or university setting is not the first thing that comes to mind when the subject of practicing anthropology is discussed. More typical are such undertakings as designing social service delivery policy in Third World countries or developing intercultural mediation systems for agencies with a multicultural clientele in the United States. Nevertheless, if we define practice as the use of the knowledge, skills, and perspectives of anthropology to help solve human problems and facilitate change, then teaching practitioners practical anthropology may be one of the most productive forms of practicing anthropology. The case of a course entitled "The Rural South" provides a good example.

"The Rural South" is a course on the culture and society of the American South offered by the Department of Sociology and Anthropology at Georgia Southern University. It was developed in response to a request from the university's Department of Nursing for a course to prepare its students to work in rural settings. The objectives of the course are to dispel among the students the stereotypes associated with the rural South, to overcome the ethnocentric bias that is common with regard to this region, to create in them some appreciation for the area's peoples and cultures, and to give them practical insights into the social and cultural dynamics of the region that will help them be more effective in their professional practice. The course combines cultural anthropology with rural sociology, taking the social problems approach of sociology and the culture area approach of anthropology. Students would need to take four separate courses ("Cultural Anthropology," "Rural Sociology," "Social Problems," and "Peoples and Cultures of the South") to cover the same ground. They would then need to synthesize the material on their own. The course is team-taught by an anthropologist and a sociologist who synthesize the material and demonstrate how it can be applied in a variety of settings.

The majority of the students who take "The Rural South" are undergraduate nursing majors. Most of the rest are education, public administration, recreation, criminal justice, and social work majors. In recent years, the percentage of nonnursing majors has grown. Majors in anthropology or sociology are a small minority of the audience. For the most part, students take the course to gain knowledge that will help them in their careers. They want the relevance of the material to be explicit, and they need to have it presented in such a way that its applications are fairly obvious. They are a pragmatic group.

The majority of the students, the nursing majors, enter the course with some misgivings. It is a required course for them, and many of them resent being compelled to take it. It is not explicitly related to the health care professions, and so they do not immediately recognize its relevance. None of this material will be on the Nursing Board tests. Finally, it is a different sort of course from those they have been accustomed to taking. Rather than focusing on a specific body of facts to be learned, it deals with abstract concepts and their use in analyzing and interpreting social and cultural phenomena. Their limited background in the social sciences leaves them poorly prepared to synthesize the material on their own or to recognize its practical applications, and so we must help them do so. We must sell most of the students on the course after they are enrolled.

The course originated in 1981 with a request from the then new Department of Nursing for our department to offer two courses that would be required in its curriculum, "Rural Sociology" and "Rural Anthropology." While the sociologists understood "Rural Sociology" clearly, the anthropologists' reaction was, "What the heck is 'Rural Anthropology'?" Several conferences with the nursing faculty revealed that they wanted both courses to prepare their students to practice in Georgia Southern's service area. The school is located in rural South Georgia and draws a considerable proportion of its students from that area. They felt that to be effective as health professionals in the rural South, nurses needed to understand more about their patients than simply their symptoms. "Rural Anthropology" turned out to be cultural anthropology with a particular emphasis on the rural South. After three years, the nursing faculty requested that the two courses be combined to eliminate overlap and free up some room in the nursing curriculum. They provided some insight on the parts of the two courses that their students had reported as the most valuable, but largely left the consolidation up to the faculty who had been teaching the old courses, the authors of this essay.

We were in substantial agreement on what the course's objectives should be, particularly that it should be oriented toward preparing professionals to practice in the rural South in a variety of settings. Health care was, of course, one of those settings. After three years of working on our own courses, we had a good idea of what we wanted to cover from our own disciplines. The sociological material tended to be oriented toward social problems while the anthropological material focused on the beliefs and values that patterned social behavior in the rural southern milieu.

Using the course objectives as a guide, we initially cut and pasted what we felt were the most important sections from the old courses into the new one. The limitations of the length of the term required that we pare our inclusions down to the essential. The integration of this patchwork into a coherent study of a regional subculture was the most challenging and creative part of the effort. We felt that to accomplish all that we wanted with the new course, team teaching would be the best approach. In order to make smooth transitions from one topic to the next, the teachers would need to be present for each other's presentations. Finally, we decided that when one of us was lecturing, the other would offer his own insights, examples, and contrasting perspectives on the topic to create a dialogue between the two instructors. Doing so would assist the students in understanding the many dimensions of the culture and society of the region and encourage them to join in the discussion. It also allowed us to interject examples of how the concepts being presented at any one time could be applied to solving problems or introducing changes. Commentary from one instructor including practical examples and case studies enhances the other's lecture and makes explicit the practical implications of the material being presented.

We began the course with an overview of critical concepts and models. Definitions of culture and of society, and the nature and causes of social-cultural change are the starting point. Branch tended to work from both the functionalist and the conflict perspective, Persico from the perspectives of cultural materialism and ecology. Branch has come to see the value of the concept of adaptation in understanding the rural South and Persico has developed an appreciation of the usefulness of functionalism in demonstrating applications for students. Both of us emphasize the importance of economy for interpreting and explaining many features of southern culture and society. This was the point of integration of Persico's adaptive approach and Branch's conflict approach. Although different, these approaches proved to be compatible and even complementary.

Race relations, for example, are approached in this manner. By using conflict as a driving force in adaptation, we could show our students the process whereby race relations in the South first developed and how and why they had changed over time to their present state. We can also show the practical implications of this relationship for health practices, education, and so forth. Sociology provides the strongest material on the social problems aspect of the subject, and anthropology provides the bio-cultural material to answer the challenges of the new versions of scientific racism that are current in our society.

One of the course requirements that has proven to be particularly valuable to the former students in work situations is an ethnographic research project. Students choose some aspect of everyday life (e.g., folk medicine, country schools, food preservation) in the rural South before World War II. They gather data through interviews with older individuals based on their memories of the period. Students typically first hate, then love the experience. From it they learn much about the traditional culture of the region, which later helps them understand clients—and many times their own family elders. An important additional benefit is skill in interviewing clients/patients for case records or medical histories. A former student who served on the advisory committee working with the instructors when the two original courses were combined urged that this feature be retained. "I did not realize it at the time, but this is the most important part of the course because it also provided me with an important practical skill," she stated.

Another student who decided to investigate moonshining for her ethnographic project reported that she had gained even more. "I had never been close to my grandfather," she related. "He always seemed distant and my parents did not encourage me to get to know him better. But when I asked him if he could help me learn about old time moonshiners, he became very excited. He knew lots of old moonshiners." She soon discovered that the old gentleman had once been a moonshiner himself and that illegal alcohol had been the foundation of the family fortune. This was a fact that his children would prefer be forgotten. "I really got to know my grandfather for the first time while working on this project," she told us. While their experiences are seldom so dramatic, many students indicate that gathering data for their research projects was the most extensive contact they have had as young adults with older people.

We next move to an overview of the cultural dimensions of rurality and of the South. Our need to deal with value orientations led us to incorporate perspectives from the symbolic approaches in both disciplines. We discuss the rural South as a "region of the mind" through an examination of defining values contained in myths told by and about rural peoples in the United States and by and about southerners and the South. It is at this point that we begin to illustrate our general discussion with specific examples drawn from current issues in the region. Values expressed in the myth of the "Lost Cause" of the defeated Confederacy and the "New South" orientation of a myth we call "Gone with the Wind" are shown to be crucial to the controversy over whether or not to remove the Confederate battle ensign from the Georgia state flag. Gradually, our students, both African American and white, come to understand why some people on both sides are ready to fight over this issue and why it was important in the 1994 Georgia gubernatorial campaign. We similarly explore these values as we survey other aspects of the culture and society such as the economy, race relations, family system, educational system, community organization, and religion. We move between broad generalizations and particular case studies to show local variations on the broad themes. We end our course with a section on contemporary social problems in the rural South and demonstrate how the material presented in the earlier sections of the course aids in understanding the problems and suggests approaches to their solution. This section includes explicit examples of how understanding the culture and society of the region can help solve problems and facilitate change in the professional areas of concern to our students.

The reaction of our students is our best measure of the success of our approach. Initially skeptical about the value of the course, they typically finish with the feeling that it was somewhat worthwhile after all. The older students who have been practicing as registered nurses with associate's degrees and who are coming back to school to earn a B.S. in nursing, however, are much more appreciative of the course. They have had experience in the workplace, and they often share experiences that point out the value of what we are teaching.

Of even greater significance is that many students return, after they have been working in the region for a few years, to tell us and others that it was one of the most valuable courses they took. For example, a former student working for a school system in South Carolina was assigned to deal with some problem cases among African Americans, who were considered to be backward and hostile to the efforts of the schools to educate their children. When she visited the students' homes, she discovered a Gullah community. She told us that she quickly recognized who she was dealing with and that many of their social patterns were just as we had described them in the course. Her insights helped her to deal with their complaints and solve the problems. Her supervisors were impressed and she was promoted.

In another case, one of the authors recently encountered a former student in her role as a charge nurse for the emergency room of a rural county hospital. She was dealing effectively and sensitively with a remarkably varied group of people needing help: older people, Hispanics, African Americans, and others. This young woman of rural origins was successfully navigating a variety of subcultural seas other than her own. She expressed her appreciation for the preparation the course had provided for those professional duties, which were not at all related to medication. The course's examination of subcultures and problems related to ageism, racism, and ethnocentrism as part of the South had given her the conceptual tools she needed to deal with people, not just symptoms.

In another case, a nurse and a former student related how the course's exploration of cultural patterns in the region had helped her deal with a particularly difficult elderly patient. His old doctor had retired and he was uncomfortable in his new doctor's office with all new staff. He was not being very cooperative with the nurse who was trying to take his case history. Our former student took over and chatted with the old gentleman for a while. She turned the conversation to family, knowing that, since she was from the area, she would find at least a distant kinship link with her patient. Once this was established, she assumed the role of a younger kinswoman. She thereby set the old gentleman at ease and no further problems were encountered. She told us that our material on family and kinship made her aware of how traditional roles could be of value in dealing with patients.

Our dean once commented in jest that so many alumni sang the praises of our course to him that he wondered how we could afford to bribe so many people. He was, of course, very impressed with these reports. We conclude that teaching practitioners practical anthropology is a practical undertaking.

Drawing the Line between People and Power: Taking the Classroom to the Community

Melinda Bollar Wagner, Shannon T. Scott, and Danny Wolfe

In an earlier essay in this volume, Michael Angrosino contends that working cooperatively with powerless communities provides one avenue to success in the field of applied anthropology. Projects that serve this goal can also, in the bargain, function as pedagogical tools and operate as "basic" research studies.

This description of two such projects will focus on the process of undertaking them, from both the teacher's and the *undergraduate* students' perspective. We will also include a small sampling of the ultimate products.

Craig County and Radford University, both located in the heart of the Blue Ridge country of Virginia, have adopted one another in a fictive kinship relationship, or at least in a symbiotic relationship. We will describe the evolution of this relationship, its problems, and its benefits.

In the spring of 1993, Radford University's "Appalachian Studies Seminar" class studied an ongoing controversy between the Appalachian Power Company (a subsidiary of American Electric Power) and citizens' protest organizations concerning a proposed 765,000 volt power line from Oceana, West Virginia, to Cloverdale, Virginia. This power line would cross Craig County, a rural county located in the Appalachian region. The county has a population of 4,372; 54 percent of its land is owned by the Washington and Jefferson National Forest.

We studied this controversy as an example of protest in the Appalachian region. Our resource people included activists from earlier environmental controversies, as well as academic experts on social movements and culture change.

The class project brought students and local citizens together. Protesters and power company executives visited the classroom and served as resource persons for students who subsequently interviewed them. Students also attended meetings of the protest organizations.

The class created a twenty-five-page script for a simulated "town meeting," with students taking on the roles of the various persons involved in the controversy. Thus, they impersonated land-owning protesters, company personnel, and representatives from the national forest and the Appalachian Trail, which would also be affected by the construction of the power line.

The script was generated by interviewing the real role players and working jointly to sift from this material the major issues the controversy raised. Each student wove the words of their interviewees together with their own words to create speeches for the town meeting. The town meeting proceeds by a point-counterpoint on each issue.

For example, a student taking on the role of a citizen from the county, with the pseudonym of "Jay Barrow," says: "My ancestors have been in the Sinking Creek area since 1754. I like it just the way it is and I don't think some big corporation should have the right to throw people off their land for the benefit of some far-off city that probably *wastes* more electricity in a day than Craig County *uses*. . . . There are still unknown *health* reasons. We have small grandchildren who play out in the yard and we don't want the lines over *them*."

Several more speeches about the health issue follow; then Mr. "James Power" from the power company is asked to comment: "We feel that no significant health effects will result from the construction of the proposed line. Our opinion is based on the fact that APCO now has over 600 miles of these lines in service and the American Electric Power system has over 2,000 miles of such lines. Some of these lines have been in service for over 20 years with no known adverse health effects nor any claims of such effects."

A thirty-minute video and simultaneous slide show were developed from the scripted town meeting (Carden et al. 1994).

The relationship between the students and their resource people wasn't always rosy. At one point our main contact, a leader in the protest group, told the teacher that he was feeling frustrated because his life had been virtually taken over by the controversy, and yet the students were attempting to study it in an objective manner for their class project. He said that the student interviewers were repeating questions that he had already answered for them in other contexts.

The debut public viewing of the video and slide show, entitled "Drawing the Line between People and Power," was at the annual Appalachian Studies Conference in March 1994. Our somewhat frustrated informant was one of the participants in our session. His reaction to the presentation showed clearly that it had turned out better than he thought it would. He was impressed with it, and it struck him on an emotional level. He had the beginnings of tears in his eyes as he watched the slides of his own and his neighbors' homes and lands that would be affected by the power line.

Students, on the other hand, were frustrated at the beginning of the project, when it was amorphous and there was no clear answer to the question, "What do we have to do [to get a grade]?" But they became engaged when we began to meet real people. When the class came to an end, students wrote journals discussing their experiences with the project. One of the students, Danny Wolfe, used these journals and his own thoughts to create a paper for the Appalachian Studies Conference. His observations follow.

When the Appalachian Studies Seminar group met for the first time on January 4, 1993, my first impression of the class and projected assignments was, "What have I gotten myself into?" "Who wants to study power lines and just how much is there to say about a power line controversy?" "Is it going to take 16 weeks?" Before long, the word *controversy* seemed to appear every time I read the newspaper or watched the news. Be it gun control, abortion clinics, landfills, or other things, the matter of the whole came to one conclusion: when people feel they are in the right and that right is being violated, they are going to fight for their cause.

When I and the majority of my classmates began this class, we knew very little about electrical power and 765,000 volt power lines. Many of us felt like we had walked into a foreign language class when introduced to the unfamiliar vocabulary of the ins and outs of the power company. When the project was completed and we reviewed what had taken place before us, most of us were now giving power line lectures to anyone who would listen. We now looked, as we drove down interstates and back roads, to see where power lines loomed and thought about *whose* land was affected so that *we* could have electricity.

The fact that we were dealing with real people and a topic that we could relate to was the key to making it a success. We tried to put ourselves into these people's shoes. What would these families do? It was a rewarding experience to talk to the actual people whose land would be affected if the power line is built. We saw and heard first-hand what would be done to the people and the land. Before the fieldwork was begun, these names were of no personal nature. They were only people living in a small rural area—people whose names were sometimes hidden in back sections of the *Roanoke Times & World-News,* but who were always on the front lines when it came to being heard and seen. Before the project and fieldwork were done, we felt a part of their lives and the wiser for having taken on this task.

In his conference paper, Wolfe (1994) noted: "Some of our classmates were outsiders to the region. It was difficult for them to understand and in some cases, appreciate the Appalachian culture. Throughout the project, this appreciation continuously progressed and many peers altered their perception of Appalachian culture."

Thus, students reported becoming aware of the politics of culture in Appalachia in a compelling way. The project worked pedagogically because students felt responsible to someone besides me, the teacher, for its ultimate success.

As we worked, the students' perceptions were that we were working as colleagues—as equals. Danny Wolfe (1994) notes, "There seemed to be no need for a leader and there was no person who took the role. Everyone provided input when they felt it was needed." We did work as colleagues; all of us were learning together. In truth, I led only occasionally.

This project served as an entree into a symbiotic relationship with the county. After our resource person had viewed the video and slides of the mock town meeting, he requested that we undertake an ethnographic study that could be used as a supplement to the environmental impact statement that is required because the power line could cross federal public lands. He asked if we could concentrate our study on the cultural attachment to land in the county.

Three students who had graduated in May 1994, three continuing students, and I became the Craig County Research Team and tackled this major research project. The research questions were: "Is there cultural attachment to land in Craig County, and if so, on what is it based?" It was at this point, then, that we began clearly doing applied anthropology, specifically in the field of cultural conservation. Certain attributes served as clues that we were now practitioners in the field of applied anthropology. For example, we had to start handing out business cards, and we were getting some pay.

Just as in traditional fieldwork, the role that we were playing was not always interpreted the same way by the anthropologists on the one hand, and by our informants or clients on the other hand. For example, I had told our major informant in a phone conversation that this kind of work was called cultural conservation. When the six students and I drove to his house to make entree and to become oriented to the county, he observed, "I know you think you have a culture to conserve here, but we have a power line to stop."

We dealt with the same issues that ethnographers face in more traditional fieldwork. For example, it was necessary to widen our sample beyond the network of the major informants; it was necessary to work in a collaborative way to discern the cultural aspects that were most salient to the residents. Our sampling, interviewing, and analysis methods had to be valid in terms of traditional research modes, or the "basic" research that we were doing to serve a specific "applied" purpose would be suspect.

The seven members of the Craig County Research Team worked as colleagues from the beginning. Some of the students had taken my course "Practicing Ethnographic Research Methods"; some of them had taken courses in Appalachian Studies; some had taken both. I asked them to teach each other what they knew in their various areas of expertise. As Shannon Scott (1995), one of the students chosen for the Craig County Research Team, notes, the "real project" experience was somewhat different from their earlier classroom experiences. Shannon says: "While most of us had done an ethnography before in a previous class, we were now doing something that was more than just studying a culture for a grade. This time we were studying a culture with a real goal in mind—finding out if there was such a thing as cultural attachment to land in Craig County. When we went into this project we knew about doing interviews and the 'joys' of transcribing, but I think many of us were surprised about the amount of time it takes to analyze data and actually get a real report together."

In the summer and fall of 1994 we interviewed seventy-eight residents, in interviews lasting from one-half hour to six hours. To help with this work, we called upon eighteen more students who were enrolled in my "Appalachian Cultures" class. For their class project, each student was given the name of a Craig County resident to interview. The eighteen students were put into six groups of three paper partners. The three students in each of these groups shared their interviews with one another; each student wrote a paper that compared and contrasted these three interviews.

Most of these students had not taken "Ethnographic Research Methods." So the original six students—the Craig County Research Team— then became the teachers and coordinators for the efforts of the "Appalachian Cultures" class. Student Shannon Scott coordinated the linking of residents with students, and handled the trouble-shooting that inevitably attends acquiring interviews from a preset sample of people. The original team came to my class to teach anthropological principles for good interviewing and to role-play interview situations. They offered themselves as support personnel. Shannon Scott (1995) describes this aspect of being a Craig County Research Team member: "We went into their class and explained that they would be helping us by going into Craig County and interviewing residents for us. Because many of these students had not done an ethnographic interview before, it was our job to teach them how to do an interview—which questions to ask, which questions to avoid and how to present themselves."

In their research papers, many in the "Appalachian Cultures" class discussed how their own views of Appalachia had changed due to the interview experience. (This was not one of the requirements of the paper but it certainly was part of my hidden agenda.) Even the original Craig County Research Team, half of whom hailed from urban areas, noted this aspect of their work. Shannon Scott (1995) says: "Through this project not only were we learning about doing anthropology, but for many of us we were learning about a new culture and seeing ruralness we had never experienced before."

The interviews yielded 1,873 pages of transcribed talk. We took 278 slides. The analysis of the transcriptions produced 1,620 pages of computerized analyses. The project's tangible products are a 92-page research report, a 30-page position paper to accompany it, several presentations by students at professional meetings (Carden et al. 1994; Scott

1995; Wagner et al. 1995b, 1995c; Wolfe 1994), and an archive of interviews that can be used by future students.

The final report, *"It May Not Be Heaven, But It's Close": Land and People in Craig County, Virginia,* begins this way:

> Picture in your mind this scene, and imagine where and when it is. A man and his wife, their friend, and a guest are seated on benches at the table in the kitchen of the couple's home. Spread in front of them is a lunch ("dinner") of thin slices of fried venison, fried chicken, biscuits baked that morning on the wood cookstove, white clover honey made by the home owner's bees, homemade cottage cheese, slaw, lime pickles, blackberry cobbler, and stewed apples. The apples are of several varieties that have been grafted by the landowner; he tells the name of each variety. In fact, all the ingredients have been raised on the land that surrounds the home, and turned into luncheon fare by the people who live here. At the end of the meal, the owner offers toothpicks that he makes out of the quill feathers of Canadian geese who stay near the pond that he built. On the wall above the doorway between the kitchen and the living room is a set of mounted deer antlers with a turkey beard hanging from each point—each feather beard bound with a gold-colored band. In the next room, a mounted bear's head rests on one wall.
>
> Where are we? What is the time period? Is this the America of the 1800s? Perhaps we are watching a scene through a window of the Explore Park, near Roanoke, Virginia, where rural American history is reconstructed. In truth, this is Craig County, June 6, 1994. (Wagner et al. 1995a)

A later section of the report describes the reciprocity among residents that the student researchers (who had recently taken the "Economic Anthropology" course) observed. "You do things for each other. If I've got something that I can do that you can't, I'd be glad to do it for you," as one interviewee told us.

Interviewees discussed neighborliness by describing classic cases of reciprocity. Reciprocity is the back and forth movement of goods and services under stimulus of obligation, in anthropological parlance, or "you scratch my back, I'll scratch yours," in more informal terms. Ever since Mauss's seminal work, anthropologists have known that the giving of gifts is not merely an economic enterprise; giving gifts creates and maintains relationships between people. Most frequently, the examples of reciprocity told to us by Craig County residents were of the balanced variety. This is the giving of goods and services with the unspoken understanding that the giver can expect to be a recipient himself in due course. This exchange is usually practiced with less close kin and with friends. For example, neighbors reported trading work in the hayfields for permission to hunt and "getting together" on prices for hay and calves.

We heard many examples of neighbors giving their garden produce to each other: "Now they are all sharing the bounty of the gardens with us; you know, they just give us a lot of stuff," as one person said. Nearly everyone has a garden (and grows more than they need), so need for produce is not at issue. As in the South American villages of the Yanomamo Indians, where arrows might be exchanged for arrows, in Craig County the gift of one kind of tomato might be returned with another kind of tomato. In both cases, the relationship that the exchange creates, maintains, and symbolizes is more important than the exchange itself. For the Yanomamo, these trading partners become allies in times of raiding. For Craig County residents, the gift givers provide advice and aid when needed and are partners in both work and play on the land (Wagner et al. 1995a).

The intangible rewards of this project include experience that students can take with them into graduate school or the work world, and sufficient good will to allow thirty more students in the upcoming "Appalachian Cultures" class to interview Craig County residents. Student Shannon Scott (1995) captured the reasons we "jumped at the opportunity" to take on the attachment to land study. Shannon says: "This project not only gave undergraduates a project to put on their resumes, but it also gave them the opportunity to get out into the field and experience what doing anthropology is really about. By getting involved in this project, students were given the opportunity to work in an atmosphere where what we did would really matter. For many of us, this was not a project for a grade but a project that allowed us to work one-on-one with our professor and gain the knowledge and self-esteem that will be needed when we move out of undergraduate school into either a career in anthropology or graduate school. This project was not done in a normal classroom setting where we were told what needed to be done. Instead we were all able to work together—students and professor—in a democratic way. Everyone's input was taken into consideration. Never did we feel like what we had to say was unimportant."

To summarize, let's evaluate whether these projects did indeed work as pedagogical tools, as research studies, and as community advocacy efforts.

They did work as *pedagogical* tools to cause undergraduate students to do extraordinary work. There are, it seems, seven reasons why they were motivating to students (Wagner 1984, 1994). First, the final products had an audience beyond just me, the teacher; second, we received grants from three different sources, symbolizing the worth of our work to outside audiences; third, we were dealing with real people, who had a real problem; fourth, the problem was one everyone could relate to, that is, it is a problem that each student could imagine happening to herself in some form in the future; fifth, we had real deadlines to meet, in order to make our work useful to the real people with the real problem; sixth, everyone's work was necessary to the whole. Any one person's undone work would create a bottleneck for the others, or make a hole in our data. The seventh and final reason is that the students were *chosen* to be members of the Craig County Research Team. Shannon Scott reported that "my self-esteem was raised, because my professor trusted me to do this work." The team members' enhanced self-esteem bore fruit in fine quality work.

That the cultural attachment to land study project worked to collect and assemble data of value as *research* is substantiated by the interest that scholars and publishers have shown in the report.

Whether the project worked as an *effort to advocate for cultural conservation* is a not-yet-answered question. The citizens' organizations are discussing whether and how to use the final products. They report being impressed by them and describe reading them numerous times. They are currently weighing the potential impact of using them in their struggle. Shannon Scott maintains that, whatever the ultimate outcome of the power line battle, the pedagogical worth of the project was worth the effort carried into it. She says, "For those of us who were involved in this project, the experience and confidence we gained will not end when the final verdict is handed down on the power line. We will carry this experience on with us and remember the time when we were chosen out of a pool of many students to step out of the classroom and into the field of real world anthropology."

She continues, "When I tell people I am an anthropology major, many respond, 'Oh, so you're going to dig in the dirt.' I then explain that there is such a thing as cultural anthropology and that I am going to study different cultures. The response I then receive is, 'Oh, so you'll be in a third world country.' I next have to explain that there are different cultures all around us to be studied. And I now know that for a fact because as an undergraduate student I practiced applied anthropology in a culture less than 30 miles from my home" (Scott 1995).

REFERENCES

Carden, Darlene H., Caryn Ergenbright, Brad Jackson, Kimberly Ledbetter Comerford, Brad Nyholm, Amy Sokoloff, Rebecca Taylor, Danny Wolfe, and Melinda Bollar Wagner. 1994. *Drawing the Line between People and Power.* Paper presented at the annual meeting of the Appalachian Studies Conference, Blacksburg, VA.

Scott, Shannon T. 1995. *Cultural Attachment to Land in Craig County, Virginia.* Paper presented at the annual meeting of the Southern Anthropological Society, Raleigh, NC.

Wagner, Melinda Bollar. 1984. Analyzing the ABCs of Appalachia: University Students Write a Children's Book. *Focus: Teaching English Language Arts* 10(2):19–25.

———. 1994. Teacher's Corner: Learning beyond the Classroom Walls: University Students Create a Children's Book. *AnthroNotes* 16(2):11–13.

Wagner, Melinda Bollar, Shannon T. Scott, Megan Scanlon, Stacy L. Viers, and Jean A. Kappes. 1995a. *"It May Not Be Heaven, But It's Close": Land and People in Craig County, Virginia.* Radford, VA: Radford University Appalachian Regional Study Center.

———. 1995b. *Documentation of Certain Intangible Elements of Cultural Heritage, Folklife, and Living Culture.* Radford, VA: Radford University Appalachian Regional Study Center.

Wagner, Melinda Bollar, Shannon T. Scott, Megan Scanlon, Stacy L. Viers, and Allyn Beth Motley. 1995c. *Cultural Attachment to Land in Craig County, Virginia: A University Project in Service to a Changing Community.* Paper presented at the annual meeting of the Appalachian Studies Conference, Morgantown, WV.

Wolfe, Danny. 1994. *Studying the APCO Line Controversy: A Retrospective on Radford University's Appalachian Studies Seminar, Spring 1993.* Paper presented at the annual meeting of the Appalachian Studies Conference, Blacksburg, VA.

The Development of Clinically
Applied Anthropology: A Cautionary Tale

Sharon Glick Miller

This is an exciting time in which to practice clinically applied anthropology. There is a growing sense of collegiality as shown by the formation of a clinical interest group within the Society for Medical Anthropology. Yet this is also a perilous time because clinically applied anthropology is at a decisive point in its development. How the goals and role of the interest group are defined may facilitate or hinder its development. I will introduce the issues at stake by first defining this area of practice.

Clinical anthropology, or clinically applied anthropology, refers to applied anthropological work in medical and mental health settings. This work includes consultation, teaching, and, in some cases, actual therapeutic intervention. The role of therapist is controversial and has been debated since the 1980 "Open Forum" on clinical anthropology in the *Medical Anthropology Newsletter.*

At present, there is a push within clinically applied anthropology toward increased professionalization as a means of "competing with credentialed professionals from other recognized clinical fields" (Johnson and Sargent 1990:9). The danger, as I see it, is that a focus on credentialing and certification will take precedence over the more difficult tasks of articulating clearly our basic assumptions and the base from which we draw, developing models that demonstrate this interconnection, and documenting the benefits that result from such application.

The need to examine the theoretical and technical foundation of clinical anthropology and the disciplinary goals supporting its application are the two core issues in the field today. I will examine them here by first telling the story of family therapy, which began as a pragmatic and critical, yet hopeful application of anthropological theory, one that was promoted with revolutionary zeal, only to lose its way as it sought professional status. I will underline the lessons this story holds for clinically applied anthropology.

BATESON REVISITED:
LESSONS FROM FAMILY THERAPY

Based on the work of Bateson, family therapy originally claimed to be not simply another clinical modality, but a different orientation. It has been described as "bursting" onto the therapy scene in the 1960s "as a breath of fresh air blowing through the musty confines of psychiatric thinking" (Schultz 1984:41). Family therapy offered a radically different view of human problems and their treatment and it articulated a paradigmatic shift in the domain of mental health. It made recurrent reference to a distinct perspective, referred to as systemic, which was congruent with an anthropological perspective (Miller 1991).

The once revolutionary ideas and practices introduced by Bateson have since become mainstream with a concomitant acceptance of family therapy; on the other hand, family therapy is more marginalized than before (Shields et al. 1994). When it was in its infancy, articles on family therapy could be found in clinical journals, and its ideas shaped clinical practice and dialogue. Now that family therapy is an established and licensed discipline, however, family therapists talk mostly among themselves in their journals, and their impact on the mainstream of psychotherapy practice is negligible.

Eager to gain professional respectability, family therapists in the 1960s, like clinically applied anthropologists today, called for a professional organization replete with a credentialing process. Sixty-seven leading family therapists advised against it, stating that this move was premature, that it would halt the generativity of the field, and would ultimately result in the credentialing of mediocrity—all to no avail. Today, family therapy is represented by the American Association for Marriage and Family Therapy, an organization that has effectively lobbied for licensure and insurance reimbursement. Its burgeoning membership has long forgotten the disaffection of those original sixty-seven leaders and takes no notice of the current disaffection of those who remember what family therapy was supposed to be. The subsequent development of specialized graduate degree programs in family therapy also raises a critical issue. Training in family therapy was originally offered following the terminal degree in a clinical discipline. It was, in essence, a perspective that could be applied to the various clinical disciplines. It now finds itself training people how to be clinicians too. The critical metaperspective that family therapy once provided has been lost. Teaching the diagnostic nomenclature needed for insurance reimbursement seems to have replaced an examination of its cultural construction.

Family therapy began as a pragmatic application of anthropological theory to clinical problems and it evolved, or dissolved, into simply another clinical modality only marginally different from the others. It therefore behooves clinically applied anthropologists to examine what happened. I will examine two key issues with an emphasis on the direction they suggest for our field: identity confusion and disciplinary differentiation.

WHAT'S IN A NAME: IDENTITY CONFUSION

Family therapy began by identifying itself primarily as an orientation and secondarily as a clinical modality. Eventually, however, these different levels became confused and subsequently were reduced to one. A similar confusion exists in clinically applied anthropology today. It is evident in the clumsy distinction made between "clinical anthropology" and "clinically applied anthropology." Clinical anthropology was a term first used by anthropologists who made no distinction between their clinical practice and their practice of anthropology. Although acknowledged to be a more cumbersome term, clinically applied anthropology has come to be preferred in that it does not imply the practice of therapy.

The distinction made between "clinical anthropology" and "clinically applied anthropology" needs to be reexamined. This dual labeling allows us to gloss over a fundamental issue that is unresolved: is there a difference and should there be a difference? Isn't clinically applied anthropology eventually put to clinical use? Also, if we agree that anthropologists are not trained to intervene clinically and that when they do it is because they also have additional training as clinicians, then why include a distinction that implies otherwise? If we do not agree, can we demonstrate that the clinical work conducted by anthropologists is different enough to be called "clinical anthropology"? My feeling is that it is not distinct enough, and we confuse paradigm with modality, as did the family therapists.

I have come to believe that when anthropologists such as myself practice as clinicians, they are not practicing anthropology, even if their practice is anthropologically informed or shaped. There are powerful constraints to clinical practice within the existing health care system in this country such that when anthropologists are conducting their clinical work with patients, it is the profession of physician, psychologist, social worker, nurse practitioner, or mental health counselor that sanctions their work.

This is not to say that for applied anthropologists to also be practicing clinicians is in itself bad. Quite the contrary! To be sure, practicing anthropologists are dependent on those outside of their applied area—both critical medical anthropologists and basic anthropological researchers—to reawaken their sensitivity to such things as the nature of power in social relations or to add the perspective unavailable to those embedded in the system. Yet at the same time, their firsthand experience adds a view that is unavailable to these others. As Bateson (1979) would remind us, it is the superimposition of different views that provides us with depth perception.

Furthermore, while a critical examination of the epistemological and metaphysical foundation of our practice is essential, our work lies in its pragmatic expression and subsequent measure of its meaning and significance. Like Bateson, who saw family therapy's goal as articulating a new epistemology for clinical practice, Lock and Scheper-Hughes (1990:71) "would like to think of medical anthropology as the key to development of a new epistemology and metaphysics of the body and of the emotional, social, and political sources of illness and healing." While it would be an error for clinically applied anthropologists to reduce their work to a clinical modality, it would likewise be an error for them to remain at the level of metaphysics at the cost of praxis. Our work is in the interface of the two.

The clinical role, especially if well conducted, also affords access and enhances credibility by introducing anthropological information in mainstream clinical journals, in core policies, and in clinical seminars, in a form in which it can be applied. It is more easily integrated into practice in this form than the occasional ancillary lecture or chapter. As Kleinman (1985:70) has said, "We need to make ourselves useful in order to make ourselves heard." Chrisman and Johnson (1990:101) have suggested that doing so means that we must "know anthropology well enough to translate it into something it was not necessarily designed for and simultaneously, to know one or another of the health sciences well enough as a cultural system to phrase this information so it will be accepted and incorporated into clinical practice."

Doing so, of course, creates a dilemma for the development of applied anthropology. If our success is measured by the integration of our ideas into existing disciplines, we must be cautious about how we separate ourselves as a practice group. In assuming the form of traditional disciplines in the clinical domain, we may become more marginally placed to achieve this goal. Again, I am suggesting that we clearly define ourselves at a different level of operation and discourse than traditional clinical practices and that we proceed with some caution in using their model of disciplinary development as our guide. It is therefore necessary to develop the discipline both internally, in terms of conceptual clarification and model development, and externally in terms of influence.

DEVELOPING THE DISCIPLINE INTERNALLY

There are few texts in clinically applied anthropology, and they provide only an elementary level of description. They function as a testimony to the clinical utility of anthropology and map the various domains of application. It is imperative that we provide a more sophisticated summary and integration of our work to date. To move forward, we need to begin by clustering our work that is now diffusely scattered among the journals of many clinical domains. We then need to analyze this work with the goal of moving beyond description to develop conceptual precision and clinically grounded model development.

To do so adequately, we need to face the issue of differentiation within this field. We want to transcend and not replicate such distinctions as those between mental and physical, primary care and psychiatry, or micro and macro levels of intervention, and so we must come to terms with our different areas of interest and influence. We need to produce texts that are more than panoramic views of the field. In order to mature as a discipline we need to organize, summarize, and build upon the base from which we draw. There is a reciprocal relationship between how we function internally as a discipline and how we are viewed externally, and so furthering our conceptual development and systematically investigating our applications will lead to greater external recognition of the discipline.

THE INVISIBLE THREAD OF ANTHROPOLOGY:
DEVELOPING THE DISCIPLINE EXTERNALLY

Anthropologists have generated a promising body of work that is extremely relevant to the clinical community and clinically applied anthropologists have succeeded in translating some of this work to the clinical realm. When we are most successful, this application is seamless. While its utility may be noted, its anthropological source is not. Furthermore, these clinically applied successes often remain unreported in our own discipline.

We need to find a way to make the thread of anthropology, now barely visible in application, as evident as a cable. We need to demonstrate better this interconnection and to evaluate the benefits that come from such application. Demonstration and evaluation is the language that our colleagues in the health sciences understand. While we may eschew positivistic notions of truth and accuracy, we can shift to constructivist notions of significance or meaning (Howard 1990). As I have already stated, in order to mature as a discipline, we need to do a better job of organizing, summarizing, and building upon the base from which we draw.

A LOOK TO THE FUTURE:
BALANCING CAUTION AND OPTIMISM

Clinically applied anthropology can be a robust discipline, but its status over time will depend on the goals and tasks it sets for itself now. While there is cause for concern with premature talk about licensure and the absence of adequate texts in the field to facilitate both training and model development, there is also cause for optimism.

There is a growing recognition, or perhaps rediscovery, of the clinical relevance of anthropology. While it is still a far cry from the wonderful interdisciplinary work of the 1940s and 1950s, there are signs of increasing interface.

First, the self-in-context is becoming a basic unit of study in both psychotherapy and culture theory as critics of current cognitive approaches to both the study of psychopathology (e.g., Coyne 1994) and the study of culture (e.g., Linger 1994) have pointed out. They note how cognition has been reduced to information processing, overlooking the construction and evocation of meaning. They call for a more sophisticated notion of self as multiple, contextualized, and culturally embedded and a more intersubjective notion of culture. Clinically applied anthropologists will play an important role in this conversation between those who wish to theorize about mind and self in this contextual way and those who wish to theorize about cultural phenomena without depersonalizing them.

Clinically applied anthropologists are also being invited into other conversations about psychotherapy. As there is more awareness of the cultural diversity within national boundaries, anthropologists are asked to address issues in the cross-cultural practice of psychotherapy. They are also invited to participate in the strong integrative movement within the field of psychotherapy, a movement that is international in scope. A study of psychotherapy integration, both within and across cultures, enhances conceptual clarity and highlights undervalued phenomena, in addition to developing more effective models.

This, too, is familiar territory for the anthropologist. In addition to the utility of a holistic perspective for this task, each theory may be viewed as a culture, as cultural process, and as product. The applied anthropologist has experience with the transfer of knowledge from one culture with its unique language and set of beliefs, values, and practices to another culture, with a different language and set of beliefs and practices. The analyses of clinically applied anthropologists pertaining to psychotherapy integration may, or more accurately, should come to play an important role in psychotherapy theory and practice.

We certainly have our work cut out for us and because of that I remain cautiously optimistic.

REFERENCES:

Bateson, Gregory. 1979. *Mind and Nature: A Necessary Unity.* New York: Bantam.

Chrisman, N., and T. Johnson. 1990. Clinically Applied Anthropology. In *Medical Anthropology: A Handbook of Theory and Method,* ed. T. Johnson and C. Sargent, pp. 93–114. New York: Greenwood Press.

Coyne, J. 1994. Possible Contributions of "Cognitive Science" to the Integration of Psychotherapy. *Journal of Psychotherapy Integration* 4:401–17.

Howard, G. 1990. Culture Tales: A Narrative Approach to Thinking, Cross-Cultural Psychology, and Psychotherapy. *American Psychologist* 46:187–97.

Johnson, T., and C. Sargent. 1990. Introduction. In *Medical Anthropology: A Handbook of Theory and Method,* ed. T. Johnson and C. Sargent, pp. 1–10. New York: Greenwood Press.

Kleinman, A. 1985. Interpreting Illness Experience and Clinical Meanings: How I See Clinically Applied Anthropology. *Medical Anthropology Quarterly* 16(3):69–71.

Linger, D. 1994. Has Culture Theory Lost Its Minds? *Ethos* 22:284–315.

Lock, M., and N. Scheper-Hughes. 1990. A Critical-Interpretive Approach in Medical Anthropology: Rituals and Routines of Discipline and Dissent. In *Medical Anthropology: A Handbook of Theory and Method,* ed. T. Johnson and C. Sargent, pp. 47–72. New York: Greenwood Press.

Miller, Sharon Glick. 1991. Some Lessons to Be Learned: Family Therapy as Applied Anthropology. Paper presented at annual meeting of the American Anthropological Association, Chicago.

Schultz, S. 1984. *Family Systems Therapy: An Integration.* New York: Jason Aronson.

Shields, C., L. Wynne, S. McDaniel, and B. Gawinski. 1994. The Marginalization of Family Therapy: A Historical and Continuing Problem. *Journal of Marital and Family Therapy* 20:117–38.

Anthropology in the Practice of Medicine

Robert C. Morrow

This essay presents two instances of anthropology applied in the practice of medicine. The first occurred when traditional beliefs interfered with the delivery of Western medical services in the Kingdom of Bhutan. The second is a study presenting what American family physicians (and comparison groups) believe are the most important attributes of a "good doctor."

GHOSTS IN THE WARD:
AN INTERCULTURAL NARRATIVE

The Kingdom of Bhutan has been and remains extremely remote (Morrow 1987). Its mountainous terrain still provides an effective barrier to the easy flow of peoples and cultures (Mehra 1974; Pommaret 1990). Only now are the traditional Bhutanese initiating contact with non-Tibetan cultures, and the government maintains tight control on the rate of change and carefully monitors the cultural effects of development projects.

In 1983 a new pediatric referral ward was established at the National Referral Hospital in Thimphu. At first, the ward experienced a not unexpected high mortality rate because patients admitted were very ill and services were limited. Whenever a child died, other parents believed that ghosts entered the area and threatened the remaining patients. As death was frequent, this belief presented problems of keeping the other families under hospital care.

The child specialist was unfamiliar with Bhutanese culture, and clinical responsibilities prevented the accomplishment of any ethnographic research. He therefore described and discussed the problem with Bhutanese colleagues and friends, and eventually word of the situation spread. His Excellency Rimpoche Dungtso Khenze became interested in the problem and requested the child specialist to consult with him. The Rimpoche approached high lamas who were socially inaccessible to the western child specialist. The Dujom Rimpoche, another renowned religious leader, provided a written blessing for the ward that was transmitted back to the child specialist by H. E. Dungtso Khenze. This blessing was framed and prominently displayed above the entrance to the pediatric ward. When fears arose among patients' families, reference could be made to the blessing, thus allaying their concerns and allowing them to remain under care.

There are many important lessons illustrated by this experience. Solutions to problems of conflicting belief cannot be provided by a clinician alone, however anthropologically sensitive or trained. The clinician must be sufficiently anthropologically competent to be able to recognize and define clearly the intercultural problems arising in the practice. Unanticipated solutions may be produced by open and frank consultation with experts from the culture in question (in this case, the Bhutanese religious leadership). Fully detailed anthropological studies are irreplaceable in determining the strength, depth, distribution, and function of beliefs in the population served. Various well-known anthropologists have worked in Bhutan, but none was available at the time of this incident. Unless we restructure the expectations, training, and functions of a clinician working in a multicultural setting, collaborative projects between the disciplines of medicine and anthropology must be promoted and funded as high priority in development projects.

ATTRIBUTES OF A GOOD DOCTOR: AN AMERICAN STUDY

The purpose of this study was to use anthropological methods to define and rank the attributes of a good family physician in the western medical practice. The aims were to generate informant-defined attributes via open-ended interviews with doctors, patients, clinic staff, and general public. The study practice was the Family Medicine Clinic of the Baylor College of Medicine Department of Family Medicine. Approval for the study was obtained from the Baylor Human Subjects Review Board.

A set of forty items for use in the structured interview stage was generated in several steps. Free-listing interviews were conducted with fifteen family practitioners randomly selected from the Harris County Medical Society membership registry, nine patients in a family practice waiting room, and five academic family practitioners from the study practice. Each respondent was asked to list all the attributes they could think of pertaining to a good doctor. These interviews yielded seventy-two commonly mentioned verbatim items, which were reduced to forty via Q sort, cluster analysis, and anthropological consultation. The Q sorts were performed by another set of family practitioners and patients not related to the study practice. The resulting forty items represented salient attributes of a good doctor drawn from a broad informant base. These items were used in the systematic data collection in the study practice and comparison groups.

The subjects of the study were faculty members of the Department of Family Medicine who were M.D.'s who provided direct patient care (N=10), patients of the same practice interviewed at the time of their doctor visit prior to being seen (N=23), medical receptionists at an unrelated urgent care center providing family care (N=7), and a neigh-borhood convenience sample of the general public interviewed at home when in good health (N=16). Each respondent ranked all forty items in a single set from "most to least important." Data were tabulated as recom-mended by Weller and Romney (1988) and analyzed via the Cultural Consensus model (Romney, Weller, and Batchelder 1986). The strength of agreement on the ranking task was measured for each of the four re-spondent groups, and a weighted answer key of the aggregate ranking was compiled for high concordance groups only. There is no theoretical justification for aggregating responses of low consensus groups. These latter data represent preference rather than cultural consensus type responses.

Physicians and receptionists were high concordance groups. The mean competency of each group as calculated by the cultural con-sensus model was .66. As a rule of thumb, above .5 is accepted as high concordance. Neither patients nor the general public showed high agree-ment on the ranking task. The weighted aggregate ranks and the an-swer keys for physicians and medical receptionists are given in Tables 1 and 2.

Physicians, not surprisingly, had high agreement on what is a good doctor. The sample was a group of colleagues in the same practice where agreement, if present, would be most likely to be found. If this

Table 1

Most Important Attributes of a Good Doctor, Ranked by Family Physician

Rank	Attribute
1	*Enjoys what he's doing, likes to practice medicine*
2	*Listens attentively to the patient*
3	*Has self-knowledge, knows the limits of his own knowledge, or when he doesn't know something*
4	Is appropriately sympathetic to patient's symptoms and makes patient feel that he cares about his pain
5	*Makes a correct and reasonable diagnosis*
6	*Is motivated to provide good care rather than by the dollar, power, or prestige*
7	Has knowledge of many facts about common medical problems, for example acne or chest pain
8	*Conscientiously follows up on abnormal test results, and maintains contact with patient until problem is resolved*
9	Is nonjudgmental and is able to suspend his own moral values in order to care for patients
10	*Has good medical intuition, gathers a lot of information and can bring it together with more than just logical thought*

Note: Attributes in italics appeared in both aggregated lists of the most important attributes to the two high-consensus groups found.

agreement extends to other family practitioners or other types of physicians, it is not discoverable by this study design.

Patients in the same practice did not have high agreement in the same ranking task. It may be that expectations are correlated with symptoms rather than with physician chosen, or may differ by demographic variables and such a subgroup analysis could not be done in a sample of twenty-three. This size is, however, large enough to detect a strong underlying consensus (Weller and Romney 1988).

The researchers did not expect to find another unrelated high concordance group: the medical receptionists in a practice independent of the study practice. Content analysis of the items in Tables 1 and 2 shows that 70 percent of the items are the same, although ranked in slightly different order. This is a high agreement out of a list of forty total items presented randomly and independently to each informant.

Table 2

Most Important Items, Ranked by Medical Receptionists

Rank	Attribute
1	*Enjoys what he's doing, likes to practice medicine*
2	*Makes a correct and reasonable diagnosis*
3	*Listens attentively to the patient*
4	Does a thorough examination
5	*Conscientiously follows up on abnormal results . . .*
6	*Is motivated to provide good care rather than by the dollar, power, or prestige*
7	*Has good medical intuition . . .*
8	Discusses the results and meanings of tests at length, taking as long as 30 minutes sometimes
9	*Has self-knowledge . . .*
10	Orders tests for medical reasons, not for financial gains

Note: Attributes in italics appeared in both aggregated lists of the most important attributes to the two high-consensus groups found.

The attributes of most import to physicians seem to be related to attitude or internal qualities (4/10) and knowledge (4/10). Only two of the items most important to medical receptionists relate to attitude, while 5/10 relate to observable physician behavior. Only two of the physician-ranked items related to observable behavior. The implications of this comparison between lists are beyond this brief presentation, but other researchers will pursue these questions of cultural content.

The important conclusion of this study is that physicians can be documented via systematic methods to be a high consensus group, and that some nonphysicians may also share in that consensus. This finding suggests that there exists a culture of good medical practice, that physicians know most about this culture, and that it can be shared by nonphysician groups. Much fascinating exploration of this culture of western healing remains for future investigations.

REFERENCES

Mehra, G. N. 1974. *Bhutan, Land of the Peaceful Dragon.* New Delhi: Vikas Publishing House.

Morrow, R. C. 1987. A Paediatric Report on Bhutan. *Journal of Tropical Medicine and Hygiene* 90:155.

Pommaret, F. 1990. *An Illustrated Guide to Bhutan, Buddhist Fort of the Himalayas.* Hong Kong: Guidebook Company.

Romney A. K., S. C. Weller, and W. H. Batchelder. 1986. Culture as Consensus: A Theory of Culture and Informant Accuracy. *American Anthropologist* 88:313–21.

Weller, S. C., and A. K. Romney. 1988. *Systematic Data Collection.* Newbury Park, CA: Sage.

Partisan Observation in the Formation of a Faculty Union: The Challenge of Organizing in a Southern Urban University

Hans A. Baer

This essay explores my role as a "partisan observer" (Caufield 1979) or "participatory researcher" (Cancian 1993) in the drive for unionization at the University of Arkansas at Little Rock (UALR). In response to a salary freeze, increased teaching loads, and restructuring proposals initiated in 1993 by the university's new chancellor, several faculty members formed the Concerned Faculty Ad-Hoc Committee, created an "underground" newsletter, and organized an election conducted by the Arkansas Department of Labor. In the latter, eligible faculty members voted to form a collective bargaining unit—the first time that such an event had ever occurred in the history of Arkansas higher education. In addition to a brief discussion of the process by which I became a critical anthropologist with a strong commitment to emancipatory endeavors at home and abroad, I present a brief account of the development of a faculty union at my university, my involvement in its establishment, and my efforts to practice anthropology by applying a critical analysis of the political economy of U.S. higher education to events at my own institution.

THE MAKING OF A CRITICAL ANTHROPOLOGIST

Although much of my anthropological research has assumed a strong theoretical slant, my decision to become an anthropologist was rooted in a loose notion of praxis, that is, a desire to merge theory and social action. As Partridge (1987:215) observes, praxis "signifies the theories and activities that affect human ethical and political behavior in social life." At any rate, the beginnings of my radicalization began not on the campus but in the corporation as an engineer. Between September 1966 and January 1970, I worked as a stress analyst for aircraft companies in Connecticut and the Seattle area. I studied engineering more out of conformity to the wishes my father, an engineer himself, the recommendations of my high school career counselors, and the *Zeitgeist* of the post-Sputnik era. I quickly experienced alienation in the highly profit-oriented aircraft industry and soothed my still politically naive conscience by telling myself that I was working on commercial rather than military projects. The ethos of the sixties eventually prompted me to study anthropology in order to comprehend the seemingly chaotic world around me and somehow play a part in making it a better place, not merely for the privileged few that flew in the 747 that I worked on, but for humanity as a whole.

Since obtaining my doctorate in anthropology, I have come to define myself as a critical anthropologist. Along with other critical anthropologists, I reject the notion of a "value-free" social science as illusory and believe that much of conventional applied anthropology all too often inadvertently serves as a handmaiden of the powers that be. Instead, I am a staunch proponent of advocacy anthropology. As Singer (1990:548) so aptly observes, "Advocacy, in the broad sense of putting knowledge to use for the purpose of social change, is the explicit aim of the anthropological endeavor. . . . The practical use of knowledge allows scholarship of a particular kind (based on an understanding of social life as a dialectical relationship between culture and history) while embracing commitment as a defining feature of anthropology."

Although I view my teaching as a form of praxis, I have attended numerous protest demonstrations over the years and have been an active member of the Arkansas Peace Center and a founder and faculty advisor of the Coalition for Peace and Justice at UALR. Within the context of one of my speciality areas, namely medical anthropology, I joined with two colleagues to co-found the Critical Anthropology of Health Caucus of the Society for Medical Anthropology. As a critical anthropologist, I have attempted to follow Laura Nader's (1972) suggestion that anthropologists "study up" as a way of understanding the plight of the "little peoples" that we have traditionally studied.

In contrast to my social activism in the larger society, I chose to minimize my involvement in campus politics, in part because I tended to view faculty governance bodies as rubber stamps for the administration. The emergence of a Concerned Faculty group during the summer of 1993 prompted me to become a partisan observer of the unionization drive on my campus. My involvement in the Concerned Faculty began in late August 1993, and since then I have kept field notes on the "faculty movement" at UALR. Throughout my involvement, I have conflated the roles of ethnographer and social activist into that of participatory research. Cancian (1993:108) provides the following succinct overview of the basic components of participatory research: "1) a commitment to the needs and interests of the community; 2) a direct engagement with the community so as to permit its problems and goals to be defined in its own voice; 3) a moral commitment to the transformation of social, political and economic injustices directly afflicting the community studied. Here, we define community in its generic sense (without neighborhood or spatial implications) as a self-conscious social unit with a focus on common identity, interests and goals."

As I reflect upon my own involvement in both the Concerned Faculty group and the UALR chapter of the Arkansas Education Association (UALR-AEA) union, I realize that I have often served as a catalyst at certain key junctures in the unionization process.

THE DRIVE FOR UNIONIZATION AT THE UNIVERSITY OF ARKANSAS AT LITTLE ROCK

Shortly after his arrival in April 1993 as the new chancellor of the University of Arkansas at Little Rock, Charles Hathaway announced the existence of a fiscal crisis related to mismanagement of funds on the part of the previous administration, as well as inadequate funding from the state legislature. He placed a freeze on salary increases of any sort and the hiring of new full-time faculty. He increased the teaching load of most faculty members who had been receiving a course reduction for research and various service activities; they were to be assigned the standard teaching load of four courses per semester. The chancellor also announced plans for restructuring the university. Four faculty members formed an informal grouping that came to be known as the Concerned Faculty Ad-Hoc Committee; they called two meetings during the summer session. Some 150 faculty members attended the first of these and about 50 people attended the second meeting. Two repre-

sentatives of the Arkansas Educational Association (AEA), an affiliate of the National Educational Association (NEA), also attended that
second meeting; their purpose was to explore the possibility of establishing a faculty union at UALR. Although NEA represents some eighty
thousand faculty members in higher education, its Arkansas affiliate had
up to that time only represented teachers and support personnel in elementary and secondary schools.

During fall 1993, the Concerned Faculty group continued to meet on
a regular basis with AEA representatives both on campus, at the home of
a faculty couple, and at the AEA headquarters; their aim was to organize
a faculty union. On September 14, 1993, the Concerned Faculty published its first issue of the *Faculty Advocate*—a newsletter that has since
appeared on a more or less regular weekly basis. The Concerned Faculty
invited the Arkansas Department of Labor to conduct an election on
the campus on December 1 and 2, 1993, for the purpose of determining
whether or not the UALR should enter into a collective bargaining arrangement with the University of Arkansas system. In an election in
which nearly 70 percent of the eligible faculty voted, the UALR faculty
voted 130 to 122 for collective bargaining. NEA/AEA was chosen in an
election in January 1994 to represent the faculty.

Despite the strong faculty sympathy for the creation of a faculty
union, UALR-AEA has found that the process of recruiting members
was an extremely difficult one. By May 1995 only some fifty faculty
members had paid the $309 annual union dues. On a more positive note,
however, UALR-AEA has recruited several staff members, despite the
fact that staff are far more vulnerable to repercussions than are faculty members, particularly tenured ones. Furthermore, the president of
UALR-AEA was elected the president of the Faculty Senate in April
1995. Despite its small size and its inability under present circumstances
to act as a collective bargaining agent, UALR-AEA has evolved into a
visible and vocal force on the campus—one that engaged in what Anto-
nio Gramsci called a "war of position" with the university administration (see Carroll and Ratner 1994). AEA and its UALR chapter were
the first to inform the faculty in Arkansas institutions of higher education
that an Arkansas State Senate committee had called for a reexamination
of the tenure policy in state universities, ostensibly on the grounds that
tenure protects "deadwood." Furthermore, UALR-AEA kept the faculty
abreast of the administration's confusing proposals for a token salary in-

crease that appeared to translate into a 1.5 percent increase over the next two academic years. Perhaps sensing a groundswell of discontent on campus, the chancellor released a memo in October 1994 announcing a somewhat larger but nevertheless inadequate pay increase—2.25 percent for classified employees and 2.00 percent for faculty and non-classified employees—effective for the period from November 1, 1994 to October 31, 1995. Despite its youth and relatively small size, UALR-AEA is a dynamic organization that in some ways recaptures the ambience of the sixties and has quickly played a much more visible role on campus than the UALR chapter of AAUP ever has.

THE MERGER OF THEORY AND SOCIAL ACTION
IN MY ROLE AS A PARTISAN OBSERVER

Although I had never previously conducted systematic ethnographic research on institutions of higher education, I have attempted to keep myself abreast of a relatively extensive critical literature on the nature of colleges and universities within the context of the U.S. political economy. As Huizer (1979:35) so aptly observes, "Part of the view *from within and from below* and the self-reflection of the social scientists should be, of course, a careful look at the institutional set-up to which they belong. This is in the first place the academic community. The place of the university, and the ideologies which it represents as an expression of the broader political economic structure, should be particularly scrutinized."

At any rate, events that led up to and eventually culminated in the formation of a faculty union at the University of Arkansas at Little Rock, where I have been teaching since 1983, provided me with an opportunity to apply my theoretical understanding of higher education to the struggle at hand. Because I was away from the campus during much of summer 1993, I did not attend the first two meetings of the Concerned Faculty group. Shortly after my return, I struck up a conversation with two of the group's organizers. They informed me that one of the more active members of the group had recently been elected president of the Faculty Senate on the grounds that he was "damn mad." He requested that the committee cancel another campuswide meeting scheduled for September 1 with AEA representatives since he wished to work for change within the faculty governance system. I argued that while perhaps the newly elected Faculty Senate president might be able to make an impact through the existing system, the Faculty Senate itself had historically functioned as a paper tiger and that the faculty should exert pressure on the administration from more than one front. One of the organizers noted later that I had served to jump-start the unionization effort.

In my outrage over the policies of the new university administration, I wrote a long personal letter about my concerns to the chancellor. Upon reading this letter in one of my classes, a student, who happened to be a reporter for the student newspaper, asked me whether I would be willing to have the newspaper publish my letter. On September 13, 1993, my letter under the by-line of "Hans to Hathaway" took up the entire second page of the student newspaper. Although the chancellor never responded to my letter in written form, many colleagues and students complimented me on its contents.

In addition to the meeting of September 1, the Concerned Faculty group met with AEA representatives on a regular basis during fall 1993, both in faculty members' homes as well as at the AEA headquarters in downtown Little Rock. I followed the lead of three other faculty members in joining AEA. I serve as the faculty advisor of the UALR Coalition for Peace and Justice, a student peace group that some students, another faculty member, and I had founded in fall 1983. In that capacity, I urged its members to organize a panel discussion on the crisis that had emerged on campus. The panel, which convened on October 20, was moderated by a student from one of my classes and included the chancellor, the president of the Faculty Senate, two members of the Concerned Faculty group, and two student members of the Coalition for Peace and Justice. While it is difficult to assess the impact of the panel discussion, it did create a public forum for publicizing the Concerned Faculty's drive for unionization.

On September 14, 1993, the Concerned Faculty launched the first issue of the *Faculty Advocate,* an underground newsletter that was renamed *Faculty/Staff Advocate* in fall 1994. The *Advocate* quickly became the group's and later the union's most effective organizing device. I have been a frequent contributor to the newsletter. As of this writing, I also serve as acting editor of the newsletter.

On September 8, 1994, I accepted an invitation from the former UALR-AEA president to serve as the Secretary of Public Affairs—a position that in a sense evolved out of my earlier involvement in the drive for unionization and is compatible with my desire to function in a more flexible capacity than is permitted by offices such as president, vice-president, secretary, and treasurer. In my role as partisan observer, during fall 1994 I also organized and chaired panel discussions on faculty unions and collective bargaining at the annual meetings of both the Arkansas Sociological and Anthropological Association and the Arkansas Educational Association.

PARTISAN OBSERVATION AS A FORM OF ADVOCACY ANTHROPOLOGY

Some time ago, Beverley (1978:83) advised radicals in higher education to take the lead in initiating union-organizing campaigns on their campuses. More recently, Neather (1993:215) has suggested that "labor and workplace struggles—including those within the university—might be a way of starting to imagine democratic spaces beyond traditional politics and even trade unions." In Gramscian terms, counter-hegemonic leadership emanates from intellectuals who maintain organic ties to subaltern groups that enable them to achieve a merger of theory and social action and of thinking and feeling. In much the same spirit, I have come to view my role in UALR-AEA in part as a "movement intellectual." This is not to say that I constitute the only "movement intellectual" in UALR-AEA. In contrast to my union colleagues, however, I have been systematically practicing anthropology in my role as a partisan observer or participatory researcher. I by no means view faculty unions as a panacea for the monumental problems faced by college and university faculty during the closing years of the twentieth century. Conversely, in keeping with my cross-cultural orientation, I draw my inspiration for collective bargaining from the victories of the labor movement in Western Europe and other industrial countries. I have come increasingly to recognize that as an academic I am an "intellectual worker" and not some sort of ill-defined professional who can freely negotiate with the university on a one-to-one basis about my work conditions.

As I reflect upon my role as a partisan observer of the struggle for unionization on my own campus and my relationship with my union colleagues, it has become increasingly apparent to me that I cannot easily separate my roles as anthropologist and social activist. Caufield envisioned the method of partisan observation to include not only the means of arriving at knowledge but also the radical alteration of the direction of flow of information and theory. Since any description of reality is necessarily incomplete, provisional, and corrigible, we should define social and cultural realities in conjunction with "the development of awareness in the community, orienting our joint studies around problem-solving projects, and including both proposals for action and action itself where such is deemed appropriate by all involved" (Caufield 1979:315).

While in my role as partisan observer I engage in many of the standard procedures, such as note-taking and informal interviews, that I have in conducting participant-observation on various groups in the United States, Britain, and East Germany. As a partisan observer, I often am not consciously aware of when I am acting as an anthropologist and when I am acting as a social activist. Despite the fact that van Willigen (1986:111) regards advocacy anthropology as "primarily a research activity" in which the anthropologist also engages in "change-producing action," these two activities have become conflated for me. My frequent assertion to my students that I am an anthropologist twenty-four hours a day has taken on a more profound reality for me as a result of my role as a partisan observer in the faculty union at my campus.

POSTSCRIPT

In spring 1995, the president of the UALR-AEA was elected president of the Faculty Senate, while I was elected as a member of the Senate for a two-year term. I have also recently become the co-editor (primarily in charge of writing) for the *Faculty/Staff Advocate*.

REFERENCES

Beverley, John. 1978. Higher Education and Capitalist Crisis. *Socialist Review* 8(6):67–91.
Cancian, Francesca M. 1993. Conflicts between Activist Research and Academic Success: Participatory Research and Alternative Strategies. *American Sociologist* 24:92–125.
Carroll, William K., and R. S. Ratner. 1994. Between Leninism and Radical Pluralism: Gramscian Reflections on Counter-Hegemony and the New Social Movements. *Critical Sociology* 20(2):2–26.

Caufield, Mina D. 1979. Participant Observation or Partisan Observation? In *The Politics of Anthropology: From Colonialism and Sexism toward a View from Below,* ed. G. Huizer and B. Mannheim, pp. 182–212. The Hague: Mouton.

Huizer, Gerrit. 1979. Anthropology and Politics: From Naivete toward Liberation? In *The Politics of Anthropology: From Colonialism and Sexism toward a View from Below,* ed. G. Huizer and B. Mannheim, pp. 3–41. The Hague: Mouton.

Nader, Laura. 1972. Up the Anthropologist—Perspectives Gained from Studying Up. In *Reinventing Anthropology,* ed. Dell Hymes, pp. 284–311. New York: Random House.

Neather, Andrew. 1993. Work and Socialist Strategy: Theory, Academics, and the Politics of Post-Marxism. *Polygraph* 6/7:212–15.

Partridge, William L. 1987. Toward a Theory of Practice. In *Applied Anthropology in America,* ed. Elizabeth M. Eddy and William L. Partridge, pp. 211–33. New York: Columbia University Press.

Singer, Merrill. 1990. Another Perspective on Advocacy. *Current Anthropology* 31:548–50.

van Willigen, John. 1986. *Applied Anthropology: An Introduction.* South Hadley, MA: Bergin and Garvey.

Building Sustainable Development at Appalachian State

Jefferson C. Boyer

In January 1991, the Sustainable Development (SD) Program at Appalachian State University began operations after a year of planning. Serving as director since that beginning, I can discuss the work of building this interdisciplinary program on our campus, with outreach to our own region and to other highland regions around the world. Both the theory and application of anthropology have much to offer sustainable development around the world. Anthropology has certainly played a key role in setting the direction for A.S.U.'s program.

DEFINITIONS OF SUSTAINABLE DEVELOPMENT

The United Nations' 1987 call for a global sustainable development represented the culmination of concerns about three linked crises that had deepened since World War II: rapid population growth; a widening gap between the wealthy and the poor; and environmental crises throughout the world (MacNeil 1989; Postel 1994). The United Nations conceptualizes SD as a process of meeting the needs of the present without compromising the ability of future generations to meet their own needs.

This concept implies a call for equity, or at least a fair distribution of the resources needed to meet human needs around the world and over time. Also implicit is the environmental issue of resource depletion or deterioration due to destructive or wasteful activities in the appropriation of resources from nature.

Our Sustainable Development Program at Appalachian is defined as a participatory process of meeting basic human needs through socioeconomic activity that does not undermine the culture of a people or the environments in which they live.

In addition to the concerns for continued reproduction, equity, and the environment, we wanted to oppose the unraveling of cultures and communities that often follows a certain kind of development. This perspective made SD directly relevant to the experience of Appalachia. We also wished to indicate that SD is primarily socioeconomic in nature, since meaningful job creation is as critical an issue in the mountains as is environmental protection. Likewise, in explicitly calling for the meeting of basic human needs, our perspective intentionally points to a path between the extremes of underconsumption among the world's poor and the overconsumption of the rich. Mountain tradition, after all, has always recognized the value of "gettin' by with what you have." Recognition of this link to local tradition facilitates acceptance of SD because it is reassuringly old as well as something new. Moreover, our program has stressed the need for widespread participation in the decisions and activities leading to a more sustainable development so that the process comes to be rooted within the community.

ANTHROPOLOGY AND SD: A THEORETICAL GOODNESS OF FIT

Anthropology's contributions to the recent conceptualizations of sustainable development necessarily take place within the context of Western epistemology and science. The etymological root of both economy and ecology is the Greek term *oikos*. For the ancient Greeks, economy was more akin to householding, that is, provisioning of the family members to assure their simple reproduction through the seasons and years. Ingemar Hedstrom (1988:8) points out that the Greeks saw the relationship between economy and ecology as analogous to the provisioning activities of the little house (economy) within the larger fluctuations of the great house or nature (ecology). Some kind of adaptive symbiosis or sustainability seems implicit in the original *oikos*. Yet with the Enlightenment, the scientific revolution, and the rise of industrial capitalism, classical and neoclassical economics and the biological science of ecology were separated (Anderson 1973:182–83). Economists such as Hazel Henderson (1991) and Herman Daly (1991a, 1991b) have made significant contributions to the SD paradigm, but they have had to do constant battle with their own field's view of nature as external to the central task of maximizing production and monetary value. Attitudes are beginning to change, but the famous law of scarcity is usually applied to financial capital, rarely to depleted stocks of natural capital. Theoretically tied to global capitalism, neoclassical economics espouses continued expansion of commodities and growth of markets and therefore has great difficulty in dealing with the critical questions of curtailed consumption, indicators of human nutrition and health, simple reproduction, and the maintenance of regional carrying capacities.

On the other side of the epistemological divide, the tendency within ecology and related biological fields has been to ignore the most active and destructive member of most biotic communities on the planet, Homo sapiens sapiens. The emerging field of conservation biology promises to break with this trend (Cox 1994). Biologists have not readily recognized that our species to a lesser or greater extent has always transformed nature and has been a part of ecosystems as we have appropriated, produced, distributed, consumed, and left waste in the process. How we do these things from here on is the crucial issue for sustainable development.

With Julian Steward's (1949, 1977) establishment of cultural ecology in the 1940s and 1950s, and Leslie White's parallel focus on humanity's ever-increasing technical capacity to appropriate nature's energy (1943, 1945), the study of human-environmental linkages has remained a central concern of American anthropology. This perspective allowed for the systematic investigation of the two "ecos," economy and ecology. Anthropology has certainly not escaped modernity's epistemological dualism: economic anthropology with its formalist, substantivist, and Marxist perspectives on the one hand, and cultural ecology, social ecology, and human ecology on the other. Nevertheless, the division has operated more as a semipermeable membrane than as a barrier. Some of the more interesting research for at least a quarter century has demonstrated the crossover effects of deforestation and desertification on human health, nutrition, lowered productivity, and agricultural yields. Analysis has also included the impacts of energy, resource, and information flows away from localities through and to global markets, and the consequences of this globalization for the sexes, the family, the community, for class and ethnicity—that is, for both social organization and consciousness. Such analyses have been produced from an economic point of view (Boyer 1979, 1984, 1987a, 1987b; Cook 1973; Cook and Diskin 1976; Gudeman 1978a, 1978b; Smith 1984, 1987; Wessman 1981) as well as from an ecological perspective (Anderson 1973; Bateson 1972; Conklin 1962; Lansing 1991; Netting 1971; Orlove 1980; Rappaport 1968, 1971). I contend that the recent proliferation of anthropological subfields has not yet occasioned a wholesale abandonment of anthropology's central enterprise: to contextualize, to attend to the part/whole relationship, to conduct holistic inquiry. As Eric Wolf (1974: 88) and many others have noted, anthropology's uniqueness and fruitfulness remains its comfortable location between things, between the sciences and the humanities, between history and literature, not infrequently to the consternation of these cognate fields. This position and insistence on grounding the enterprise in cross-cultural fieldwork has enabled anthropology to make several contributions to SD, including, but certainly not limited to, the following ideas.

1. The ancient Greeks were right: the human activity we call economic and the realm of the ecological are conjoined, regardless of modernity's efforts to separate them in theory and practice. Conceptual frameworks in political economy and human ecology form an *oikos* around questions of social and natural reproduction, or, as I say in class, the capacities of people and social systems within ecosystems to "keep on keepin' on" (Boyer 1979, 1984, 1987a, 1987b; Cook 1973; Godelier 1972; Orlove 1980).

2. All human activity within the double dialectic of people-people relations or human-nature relations is mediated through consciousness, and human consciousness, involving perception, cognition, and emotion together build world views that can be both astoundingly accurate and yet blind. Whether we are concerned with the sophisticated ethnobotany of the Philippine Hanunoo, who distinguish fifteen hundred plants and plant parts (Conklin 1962:19) or with the perceptions of inner city American youth for whom environment means asphalt, concrete, crack cocaine, and an occasional house plant, we approach reality through a cultural filter. It is our biological nature to be cultural, to spin out the webs of meaning and forests of symbols and to relate to the world by such means. To mystify, fetishize, and create false consciousness (Marx 1964, 1967; Marx and Engels 1970), to thingify and atomize continuities (Taussig 1980), and to be blinded to the systemic nature of

individual, society-nature relationships, whether through the sedimentations of cognitive consciousness or arrogant hubris (Bateson 1972), seems to be part of what it is to be human. How people can learn and enact more adaptive behaviors, to become more ecocentric and perhaps less anthrocentric, seems possible but always within the limits of this curious twist of human nature and "minding" that humanizes all phenomena, whether social or natural. Too often the proponents of ecocentric approaches (Eckersley 1992), "biophilia" (Orr 1994; Wilson 1984), or the hypothesized coming ecozoic age (Berry 1988) miss these anthropological insights most clearly demonstrated in Gregory Bateson's pioneering *Steps to an Ecology of Mind* (1972). Bateson shows how consciousness and symbolic representations of the natural, material world, whether reified or accurate, help to construct personal and emotional experience as well as religious, cosmological, and philosophical realms. Indeed, even such ideational cultural institutions often reveal much about the material sustainability of a society over time.

3. The insight, shared with history and other social sciences, that consciousness and behavior are profoundly influenced by the particular economic and social formation in history that accompanies them. Capitalism, for example, did not invent greed or exploitation, but it certainly has encouraged certain forms of both within modern and postmodern cultures (Godelier 1972, 1977; Marx 1967; Weber 1947). Even if one disputes the particulars of his typology, Marshall Sahlins's classic "Poor Man, Big Man, Rich Man, Chief" (1990) demonstrates that one can inquire about the appropriate norms, values, and behaviors only with reference to the particular social system. By extension, gender, ethnic, and class stratifications must also be taken into account. Therefore, future sustainability must not only be concerned with forms of thinking, but also with more cooperative forms of association and economic activity, moving toward the development of more eco-sensitive social and economic systems from the local and regional to national and global levels. It is worth noting here that Lansing's study (1991) of Bali's ancient systems of water temples and priest-directed water works linked significant social hierarchy and complexity with environmental sensitivity. This process involves both centralized and decentralized decision making and serves to restrain facile assumptions that sustainable social systems are always simple, always "Paleolithic," and can only operate at band or tribal levels.

4. Anthropological studies of gender and ethnicity around the world demonstrate that it is women who are primarily involved with family nurturing and householding, and that native peoples masterfully conserve fragile ecosystems even as they live from them. Beset by the global forces of macro-development, women and native peoples both need outside support to survive but they also provide models for a more sustainable development (Jacobson 1993). The new "women in development" field brings into clear focus strategies of mutual support, micro enterprises, and family planning that challenge contemporary patriarchal institutions that neither nurture nor allow women to gain control of their own bodies and reproduction. At the same time, wilderness and fragile lands conservation strategies, essential for the protection of the remaining biodiversity, are increasingly involving native peoples whose ancestral homes are the threatened rain forests, wetlands, or deserts (Denniston 1994; Durning 1993). Anthropological contributions to strategies of resource conservation and SD are clear and unmistakable (Hardenbergh 1992, 1993; Quiatt and Koester 1994).

5. Current studies of peasants, changing economic systems, cities, gender, health and educational systems, and human ecological research increasingly involve topics crucial to SD, such as the role of nongovernmental organizations (NGOs) in local, regional, and national policy making and development strategies. Anthropologists have invaded the territory traditionally occupied by political scientists, economists, and geographers as they have occupied ours. The result can only be an enriching cross-fertilization of ideas regarding theory, method, and strategies for greater SD (Horowitz 1994). The foregoing should make it clear that anthropological theory has much to say about the continued reproduction of living systems, Homo sapiens included, about the equity or inequity of particular developmental forms, and about respecting the human as well as the biotic community.

CREATING THE SD PROGRAM AT APPALACHIAN STATE

In August 1990, I returned to Boone after leading a work/study internship with A.S.U. students in southern Honduras near the Nicaraguan border where I had conducted doctoral research. We witnessed firsthand the consequences for the peasant highlanders of thirty years of deforestation brought about by export agriculture and steady population

growth. Also visible were the effects of the recent Contra War in the
border towns and hinterlands. Without calling it that, the *campesinos*
talked a lot about SD notions, about the need to conserve soil, water, and
the remaining forests in their own agriculture and economic activities
(Boyer 1991). Dr. Dennis Scanlin, who teaches "Appropriate Technology" in the Technology Department, visited us during the last week and
brought in his backpack a demo solar oven for cooking without firewood
and a ram pump for small-scale irrigation without the need of fuel for
pumping. Both technologies interested the villagers, the Catholic Relief
Program heads, and, in Tegucigalpa, the representatives of grassroots
development organizations. We planned for a national solar education
project, involving the local NGOs in seven regions of Honduras and
A.S.U. within two years.

This project with Scanlin and conversations with Dr. Loren Raymond, an A.S.U. geologist who also headed a small interdenomina-
tional foundation, the Ecumenical Project for International Cooperation
(EPIC), led us to brainstorm about an SD program that would be both a
program of study and a series of projects in our mountain communities
with outreach to other highland regions like southern Honduras. I recall
that the one-page proposal to establish the SD Program shook in my
hands as I broke rank and went straight to the chancellor's office in late
August. Fortune smiled. It so happened that Chancellor John Thomas
was looking for ways to advance environmental studies and ways to
internationalize our curriculum and campus. He arranged for a meeting with the provost, key vice-chancellors, deans, and program heads
in early September. With their authorization, we (Boyer, Raymond, and
Scanlin) worked for a semester to plan for an interdisciplinary undergraduate minor, a graduate concentration, and community projects focused on various aspects of SD. The dean of Arts and Sciences, the
college that encompasses all interested departments except for the Technology Department, was particularly supportive; he authorized the program director position. As Raymond, Scanlin, and I scheduled meetings
with five departments, the head of Appalachian Studies, three deans and
two additional vice-chancellors that fall, we patiently demonstrated our
plans, emphasizing how the new SD program would be academically
rigorous, involve all interested faculty, and work on real world problems in the wider community. We agreed to establish a program director
answerable to an advisory board composed of approximately twelve

interested faculty from across the departments, disciplines, and colleges. The key units were anthropology, biology, geography and planning, geology, interdisciplinary studies, technology, and Appalachian studies. Also needed was an administrative home for the program. Since a new faculty position for the director was necessary, and since I applied for and was offered the position, and since the Anthropology Department actively supported this new initiative, it was decided to link SD administratively to the Anthropology Department. As director, I would teach one of the two required courses for the minor ("SD in the Modern World System"), teach two more anthropology courses, and (with a quarter-time release) direct the program. The late Father Thomas Cowley, a British Dominican priest and campus minister who had previously served A.S.U., had founded EPIC and had created a library with journals on human rights, environmental studies, international grassroots development, and peace studies. Dr. Raymond and the EPIC board decided to donate the library and supportive funds to the new SD Program.

I began teaching the SD course in spring 1991, with twenty-six undergraduates and two graduate students from Technology. Since then the number of undergraduate minors has reached approximately ninety students with five graduate students in the SD concentration (from Political Science, Education, Biology, and Technology, the Anthropology Department not currently having a graduate program). Set at a senior undergraduate and graduate level, I originally designed the SD course for seminar size. It now attracts more than thirty students both fall and spring semesters.

At the core of the SD curriculum are the following courses: my SD course, "Society and Technology" taught by Scanlin, along with courses on solar and other alternative technologies, ecology courses, world regional geography and regional planning courses, a science and culture course, and peace studies. In addition we are instituting an environmental geology course. Two new additions to our faculty, a Latin American geographer and an economist specializing in the Caribbean, will give a needed "women in development" focus to our core curriculum. This year I have also experimented with an interdisciplinary, team-taught "humans and global change" course at the introductory level. The minor consists of eighteen hours of required courses: the SD course and society and technology required courses, three elective courses, and one three-hour practicum (a laboratory, shop, or work/study internship course).

One of the more popular innovations has been the addition of a sustainable agriculture component to the program, thanks to the donation of a thirty-acre hillside farm in nearby Cove Creek. Agroecologist Bryan Green, who had Peace Corps experience among highland Philippines farmers, was hired. He provides students academic courses and hands-on internship experience through two growing seasons. Terracing methods from the Philippines and Honduras have shown students the possibility of highland-to-highland reverse technology transfer. In addition, the newer principles of permaculture and older, sustainable methods of Appalachian farmers are used in teaching, research, and demonstration. Green also began to work with local farmers and consumers in a subscription system for the production, sale, and consumption of fresh, organic produce.

Outreach to the community began with a Z. Smith Reynolds Foundation grant to study our regional economy with an eye toward greater sustainability (Boyer, Monast, and Moretz 1993). The same foundation funded us to bring in members of the Rocky Mountain Institute, who conducted a citizen's workshop on sustainable economic renewal. The result was the creation of the Watauga Coalition for Sustainable Development, a body that sponsored an energy efficiency workshop and is planning a workshop for rural job creation and land use projects. Students have helped this outreach through researching citizens' attitudes about protecting water quality and composting, and by interning in a state and county waste management program and with the Blue Ridge Environmental Defense League (Boyer 1993:10). Anthropologist and board member Harvard Ayers has been instrumental in finding internships for students in the Southeast and Southwest and in providing material support through his national connections with the Sierra Club. He has also become the informal advisor to the active environmental student organization. Without taking undue credit for recent student initiatives for environmental stewardship, it is worth noting that the leaders of the student environmental organization that attempted to save Howards Knob and support the Boone alternative transportation plan (Healy 1995), won the student government election for the 1995–96 academic year; they also supported Hunter Schofield, who became the first student to be elected to Boone's Town Council. Almost all these students are SD minors.

Part of the program's strength is its world regional focus that begins at home in southern Appalachia and extends to ongoing agriculture, health care, and small business projects in the southern Honduran highlands. In 1992, Scanlin and I returned with seventeen students and successfully completed the national solar education and demonstration project in five regions of the country. In the summer of 1995 a barefoot doctor training program took sixteen students back to Honduras along with Bill Herring, M.D., a wilderness medicine expert. All of this work in Honduras is based on my ethnographic research as well as the contacts built up over a thirty-year period that began with Peace Corps service in the early 1960s. In addition, Dr. Nick Biddle (History and SD board member) has just established exchanges with a new rural university in Ecuador for Quechua speakers in the Andes; the university has requested help with a sustainable development curriculum (Biddle 1995). We have also visited Mexico, the Carpathian region of central Europe, and rural Ireland, investigating the possibility of future collaborative exchanges.

Although the present struggles in the state over the future funding for higher education loom as a dark cloud, we do think that our program has made a good start. Our long-range goal is to establish an M.A. program in Environmental Studies and SD for professional practitioners. Certainly anthropology will have an important role in training to conduct cultural acceptability and social impact assessments, community needs assessments, rapid rural appraisal and political economic research at local and regional levels. Our niche would be to contribute to the research, teaching, and catalyzing SD in rural highland regions.

REFERENCES

Anderson, J. 1973. Ecological Anthropology and Anthropological Ecology. In *Handbook of Social and Cultural Anthropology,* ed. J. Honigmann, pp. 189–239. Chicago: Rand McNally.

Bateson, G. 1972. *Steps to an Ecology of Mind.* New York: Ballantine.

Berry, T. 1988. *Dream of the Earth.* San Francisco: Sierra Club Books.

Biddle, N. 1995. Keeping the Experience Alive: Sustainable Development and A.S.U.'s Andean Study Program. Paper presented at the Sixth Annual Conference of the Association of Academic Programs in Latin America and the Caribbean, Knoxville, TN.

Boyer, J. 1979. From Burning to No Burning: Some Structural Constraints on Traditional Agriculture and Economic Rationality in Southern Honduras. Paper presented at the annual meeting of the American Anthropological Association, Cincinnati.

———. 1984. From Peasant Economia to Capitalist Social Relations in Southern Honduras. *Southeastern Latin Americanist.* 27(1):1–22.

———. 1987a. Capitalism, Campesinos, and Calories in Southern Honduras. In *Directions in the Anthropological Study of Latin America: A Reassessment,* ed. J. Rollwagen, pp. 3–24. Albany: State University of New York Press.

———. 1987b. Que Hay en la Bodega? Vanishing Reserves of Peasant Economia in Southern Honduras. Paper presented at the annual meeting of the Southeastern Conference of Latin American Studies, Merida, Mexico.

———. 1991. Is Sustainable Agriculture and Development Possible in Southern Honduras? Paper presented at the international conference "Varieties of Sustainability?" Santa Cruz, CA.

———. 1993. Sustainable Development at Appalachian State University: Opening Minds to *Oikos. Oikos* 1(3):8–11.

Boyer, J., J. Monast, and R. Moretz. 1993. *Toward a Sustainable Economy in Western North Carolina: Ashe and Watauga Counties. Report for the Community.* Boone, NC: Z. Smith Reynolds Foundation, Sustainable Development Program, Appalachian State University.

Conklin, H. 1962. The Study of Shifting Cultivation. *Current Anthropology* 2:27–61.

Cook, S. 1973. Economic Anthropology: Problems in Theory, Method, and Analysis. In *Handbook of Social and Cultural Anthropology,* ed. J. Honigmann, pp. 795–860. Chicago: Rand McNally.

Cook, S., and M. Diskin, eds. 1976. *Markets in Oaxaca.* Austin: University of Texas Press.

Cox, G. 1994. *Conservation Ecology: Biosphere and Biosurvival.* Dubuque, IA: W. C. Brown.

Daly, H. 1991a. *Steady State Economics.* Washington, DC: Island Press.

———. 1991b. Sustainable Growth: A Bad Oxymoron. *Grassroots Development* 15(1):39.

Daly, H., and J. Cobb. 1989. *For the Common Good.* Boston: Beacon Press.

De la Court, T. 1990. *Beyond Brundtland: Green Development in the 1990s.* New York: New Horizons Press.

Denniston, D. (with Mac Chapin). 1994. Defending the Land with Maps. *World Watch* Jan./Feb.:27–31.

Durning, Alan. 1993. Supporting Indigenous Peoples. In *State of the World, 1993,* ed. L. Brown, pp. 80–100. New York: W. W. Norton & Co.

Eckersley, Robyn. 1992. *Environmentalism and Political Theory: Toward an Ecocentric Approach.* Albany: State University of New York Press.

Godelier, M. 1972. *Rationality and Irrationality in Economics.* New York: Monthly Review Press.

———. 1977. *Perspectives in Marxist Anthropology.* London: Cambridge University Press.

Gudeman, S. 1978a. Anthropological Economics: The Question of Distribution. *Annual Review of Anthropology* 7:347–77.

———. 1978b. *The Demise of a Rural Economy: From Subsistence to Capitalism in a Latin American Village.* London: Routledge and Kegan Paul.

Hardenbergh, S. 1992. Realizing Conservation-Development in Madagascar. *Valley Optimist* 1(8):8, 9, 38.

———. 1993. *Undernutrition, Illness, and Children's Work in an Agricultural Rainforest Community of Madagascar,* Ph.D. dissertation, University of Massachusetts.

Healy, T. 1995. Mountain Piques ASU Debate. *Raleigh News & Observer,* Jan. 31:1A, 8A.

Hedstrom, I. 1988. *Somos Parte de Un Gran Equilibrio: La Crisis Ecologica en Centoamerica.* San Jose, Costa Rica: Departamento Ecumenico de Investigaciones (DEI).

Henderson, H. 1991. *Paradigms in Progress: Life beyond Economics.* Indianapolis: Knowledge Systems.

Horowitz, M. 1994. Development Anthropology in the Mid-1990s. *Development Anthropology* 12(1&2):1–14.

Jacobson, Jodi. 1993. Closing the Gender Gap in Development. In *State of the World, 1993,* ed. L. Brown, pp. 61–79. New York: W. W. Norton & Co.

Lansing, S. 1991. *Priests and Programmers: Technologies in the Engineered Landscape of Bali.* Princeton: Princeton University Press.

MacNeil, J. 1989. Strategies for Sustainable Economic Development. *Scientific American* 9:155–65.

Marx, K. 1964. *The Economic and Philosophic Manuscripts of 1844.* New York: International Publishers.

———. 1967. *Capital: A Critique of Political Economy.* New York: International Publishers.

Marx, K., and F. Engels. 1970. *The German Ideology.* New York: International Publishers.

Netting, R. 1971. *The Ecological Approach in Cultural Study.* Boston: Addison-Wesley.

Orlove, B. 1980. Ecological Anthropology. In *Annual Review of Anthropology* 9:235–73.

Orr, D. 1987. *Our Common Future: The World Commission on Environment and Development.* New York: Oxford University Press.

———. 1994. *Earth in Mind: On Education, Environment and the Human Prospect.* Washington, DC: Island Press.

Postel, S. 1994. Carrying Capacity: The Earth's Bottom Line. In *State of the World, 1994,* ed. L. Brown, pp. 3–21. New York: W. W. Norton & Co.

Quiatt, D., and S. Koester. 1994. Resource Conservation and Sustainable Development: Anthropology's Contribution. *Opinion. National Geographic Research and Exploration* 10(2):139–40.

Rappaport, R. 1968. *Pigs for the Ancestors: Ritual in the Ecology of a New Guinea People.* New Haven: Yale University Press.

———. 1971. Ritual, Sanctity, and Cybernetics. *American Anthropologist* 73:9–76.

Sahlins, M. 1990. Poor Man, Big Man, Rich Man, Chief. In *Conformity and Conflict: Readings in Cultural Anthropology,* 7th ed., ed. D. Spradley and R. McCurdy, pp. 334–48. Glenview, IL: Scott, Little, Brown Higher Education.

Smith, C. A. 1984. Local History in Global Context: Social and Economic Transitions in Western Guatemala. *Comparative Studies in Society and History* 26:193–228.

———. 1987. Regional Analysis in World System Perspective: A Critique of Three Structural Theories of Development. *Review* 10:597–648.

Steward, J. 1949. Cultural Causality and Law: A Trial Formulation of the Development of Early Civilizations. *American Anthropologist* 51:1–27.

———. 1977. The Concept and Method of Cultural Ecology. In *Evolution and Ecology: Essays on Social Transformation,* ed. Jane C. Steward and Robert F. Murphy, pp. 43–47. Urbana: University of Illinois Press.

Taussig, M. 1980. *The Devil and Commodity Fetishism in South America.* Chapel Hill: University of North Carolina Press.

Weber, M. 1947. *The Theory of Social and Economic Organization.* New York: Free Press.

Wessman, J. 1981. *Anthropology and Marxism.* Cambridge, MA: Schenkman.

White, L. 1943. Energy and the Evolution of Culture. *American Anthropologist* 41:556–73.

———. 1945. Diffusion vs. Evolution: An Anti-Evolutionist Fallacy. *American Anthropologist* 47:339–56.

Wilson, E. 1984. *Biophilia.* Cambridge, MA: Harvard University Press.

Wolf, Eric. 1974. *Anthropology.* New York: W. W. Norton and Co.

Practicing Anthropology in the Carter Presidential Center

Honggang Yang

I first came to the American South from the People's Republic of China in 1986, as a student of applied anthropology. After the completion of my doctoral course work at the University of South Florida (USF), I started an internship that was a part of the training requirements. My internship project took the form of ethnographic fieldwork focusing on the disputing processes involving the management of the commons by a homeowners association in Tampa (Yang 1992a). This research formed the basis for my dissertation.

Upon graduation from USF, I started my job hunting and in the early fall of 1991, I was invited to interview for a position at the Carter Presidential Center in Atlanta. Over the past decade, the Carter Center has received more and more public recognition and has become a symbol of commitment to global peace. I was thrilled when I was hired as a research associate in the conflict resolution program there. Later I learned that it was my cross-cultural knowledge and applied anthropological training in the fields of peacemaking and conflict resolution that had attracted their interest in me.

As an organization, the Carter Center is a nonprofit, nonpartisan public policy institute that former President Jimmy Carter founded in 1982. The Center is home to a group of organizations that unite research and outreach applications. Its core organization is the Carter Center of Emory University (CCEU). Apart from the projects on international health policy, global development, African government, Latin America, and the United States, conflict resolution and human rights are the two principal foci at the Center (Yang 1993a). In this paper I will draw upon my working experience and observations and reflections at the Center in the past few years to illustrate the challenges now facing anthropologists' involvement in practical issues of peace and conflict resolution.

President Carter's conflict resolution work is based in large part on his experience at the Camp David Peace Talks in 1978 (Babbitt 1994). The resolution of internal, armed conflict is currently his central focus, since the majority of the armed conflicts now are civil wars taking place within national boundaries. Many violent conflicts, Carter believes, are derived from basic human rights violations. But a disservice is done to understanding human rights by constant reference to the United States as the model of a rights-protective society; more reference should be made to the smaller Western social democracies that have longer traditions of protection of civil, political, and economic rights (Howard 1990). Carter recognized this position and initiated his Atlanta Project to address these domestic social issues in 1992.

Disputing parties caught up in costly conflicts had nowhere to turn when they needed assistance in finding nonviolent means to resolve their problems. This lack of recourse was due to the prohibition, restriction, limitation, and constraint of the powers of the international and regional organizations. It was in this complex context that the International Negotiation Network (INN) was developed to fill the identified mediation gap and in which my work was concentrated at the Carter Center.

The INN was initiated by Carter, together with other international leaders, in 1987. They envisioned a growing need for a new approach to the resolution the many internal conflicts now found in the world. Overseen by a council of "eminent persons" and a group of experts and practitioners, the INN's approach involves third-party mediation, especially "eminent mediators."

Throughout the implementation of the CCEU programs, the "eminent persons" strategy has been used to get the parties to the table. This strategy has some special characteristics: immediate access to leaders, experts, and data; ability to mobilize resources and borrow infrastructure support without the usual attendant organizational encumbrances; and mass media attention to promote the negotiation environment.

The role of eminent persons in third-party mediation is perhaps the most important characteristic of the INN approach. As a former head of state, Jimmy Carter has access to virtually anyone in the world. His phone calls are always accepted. When he needs assistance, people in various sectors respond (Spencer, Spencer, and Yang 1992). Jimmy

Carter has the trustworthiness, credibility, mediation experience and ability, and charismatic authority to persuade the parties to go to the negotiation table. There are very few other world figures who share these attributes. At the same time, the role of any individual is limited by his or her personal, sociocultural, or political background, morality, and acceptability to the parties in a particular context.

In addition, there are some special considerations that shape the CCEU/INN involvement, namely: (1) there should be a mediation gap; (2) duplication or competition with other organizations should be avoided; (3) the invitations have to come from all the parties; and (4) considerations must be given to the timing of third-party assistance. At the Center, we monitored existing and emerging armed conflicts; convened confidential consultations for disputants and mediators; matched disputants' needs with potential third parties, funding sources, and experts; and performed pre-mediation services that included analysis of the issues, generation of options, and building of trust. During my tenure at the Center we held two major consultations to spotlight internal armed conflicts and to set forth action agendas through a strengthened use of nongovernmental and intergovernmental actors (Yang 1993b).

My working role as an applied anthropologist entailed the research and delivery of the third-party assistance (e.g., mediation, facilitation, election monitoring/observing, or convening of the negotiations) based on a cross-cultural understanding of armed conflicts in a complex, international context. In 1993 I also became the coordinator for the internship program on conflict resolution. The collection and provision of information has long been a crucial part of the day-to-day operations at the Center and student interns play important roles in providing the information resources. As director of the internship program, I organized a round table for student interns who gathered the information and provided the weekly updates and encouraged them to think creatively but realistically.

Weekly updates of conflict situations and developments are critical to the Center's work. Compilations of the updates are distributed to the INN Council and core group members, and they cover information on peace attempts, armed conflicts, elections/politics, human rights, humanitarian issues, refugees, and foreign aid. A major source of the information for the updates is the Lexis/Nexis on-line services (Yang 1993a). Ethnographic data were among the things that I took particular care in reviewing and providing. Bias and one-sidedness exist in mass media reports, which therefore need to be balanced with ethnographic, holistic, in-depth, field knowledge. There is a problem with straight ethnographic data, as ethnographic documents are often very lengthy and filled with detailed descriptions of everyday life. Nevertheless, many anthropologists did their fieldwork in areas where ethnic disputes and human rights violations now prevail, enhancing the value of those ethnographic documents. It was quite a challenge to make use of these ethnographic materials in a context where rapid developments require quick responses to emerging concerns. In this connection, I suggested (Yang 1992b) that anthropologists pay more attention to the national character studies three years ago, despite the reluctance of many anthropologists to express sociocultural themes beyond particular local or topical boundaries. Of course, empirical generalizations are always defined by their corresponding limitations in concrete contexts. Our research tradition values variations and diversities in conceptualization. Hsu (1983) is right that the anthropologist often has to comment on national societies as wholes, either from scientific or practical reasons, because human issues cannot be understood by descriptions of the marriage customs or age-grading practices in single villages or tribes. From my own experience at the Carter Center, I was often asked to suggest short-term solutions and immediate action steps despite an imperfect understanding of the holistic elements of the culture of the disputing parties (Yang 1994). In my opinion, anthropologists must overcome their reluctance and hesitation to say what they know and what they experienced in the field, regardless of the limitations.

One additional role I fulfilled at the Carter Center was that of an advocate for non-Western, indigenous approaches to addressing the issues of conflict and peace, since the Western mode of dispute settlement dominates (Yang 1993b). I wanted to increase the use of ethnographic knowledge in the field; as a result, I tried to get more anthropologists involved in this work and to make more cross-cultural references in the information gathering and reporting at the Center. There are, however, challenges in advocating the indigenous methods of conflict management, since communally oriented systems of social justice, based on ascribed and differentiated memberships in small-scale pastoral or agricultural societies, unfortunately cannot be, as Howard (1990) points out, transferred to the modern, large-scale state arena. A central, practical question I worked on at the Carter Center was how the indigenous perspectives of peace and grassroots devices of conflict settlement can be better understood within a holistic context and made more applicable, more efficient, and more widespread in peacemaking and conflict resolution.

There are many happy memories for me about my three years at the Center, especially those times when I worked directly with former President Carter. I still remember vividly the time he tried to pronounce my first name when he was visiting Center staff members in their offices. There is a good feeling inside me when I remember the speech I helped to draft that he gave to a United Nations meeting via telecommunication media. And I am filled with pride when I remember when he shook my hand after he had used some briefing materials I had prepared for him prior to a meeting with a Sudanese delegation. He said to me with his warm smile, "Thank you for your help."

I was honored to work for him.

REFERENCES

Babbitt, E. F. 1994. Jimmy Carter: The Power of Moral Suasion in International Mediation. In *When Talk Works,* ed. D. M. Kolb and Associates, p. 376. San Francisco: Jossey-Bass.

Howard, R. E. 1990. Group versus Individual Identity in the African Debate on Human Rights. In *Human Rights in Africa,* ed. A. A. An-Na'im and F. M. Deng, pp. 159–83. Washington, DC: The Brookings Institute.

Hsu, F. L. K. 1983. The Cultural Problem of the Cultural Anthropologist. In *Rugged Individualism Reconsidered: Essays in Psychological Anthropology,* ed. F. L. K. Hsu, pp. 420–38. Knoxville: University of Tennessee Press.

Spencer, D., W. Spencer, and H. Yang. 1992. Closing the Mediation Gap: The Ethiopia/Eritrea Experience. *Security Dialogue* 23(3):89–99.

Yang, Honggang. 1992a. Preserving the Commons in Private Cluster-Home Developments. *Practicing Anthropology* 14:2:9–11.

———. 1992b. The Practical Importance of National Character Studies. *Southern Anthropologist* 19:2.

———. 1993a. Operation of the Conflict Resolution Program at the Carter Center. Paper presented at the annual meeting of the Peace Studies Association, University Park, PA.

———. 1993b. The Practical Use of Ethnographic Knowledge: Face-Saving Devices in Conflict Resolution. Paper presented at the National Conference on Peacemaking and Conflict Resolution, Portland, OR.

———. 1994. Keeping the Ethnographic Knowledge Current. Paper presented at the annual meeting of the American Anthropological Association, Atlanta.

Contributors

MARY K. ANGLIN is an assistant professor of anthropology at the University of Kentucky, where she holds a joint appointment in the Department of Anthropology and the Department of Social and Behavioral Science in the College of Medicine. Her research interests include breast cancer, HIV/AIDS, women's health, and access to health care, as well as political, economic, and gendered analyses of Southern Appalachia.

MICHAEL V. ANGROSINO is a professor of anthropology at the University of South Florida. He has been involved in the development of training programs for applied and practicing anthropologists since 1973, and has served as editor of *Human Organization,* the journal of the Society for Applied Anthropology. His professional interests include mental health policy and the assessment of services for persons with mental retardation and chronic mental illness.

HANS A. BAER is a professor in the Department of Sociology and Anthropology at the University of Arkansas at Little Rock. He has research interests in Mormonism, African American religion, critical medical anthropology, medical pluralism, and the sociopolitical conditions in East Germany both before and after the unification. He recently completed a research project on the status of the churches in the new German states for the Life and Peace Institute in Sweden. His most recent book, co-authored with Merrill Singer, is *Critical Medical Anthropology* (Baywood, 1995).

JEFFERSON C. BOYER is an associate professor of anthropology and director of the Sustainable Development Program at Appalachian State University. He is an ethnologist specializing in peasantries, social movements, and rural development, concentrating on Central America. Since the 1970s he has consulted on agrarian reform and village health care in Honduras and Costa Rica. Since establishing the sustainable development program at ASU, he has been working on development issues in southern Appalachia.

ROGER G. BRANCH is a professor of sociology and chair of the Department of Sociology and Anthropology at Georgia Southern University. He has teamed with Dr. V. Richard Persico Jr. to teach the course "The Rural South" for the past eleven years. As a social scientist in predominantly rural southeastern Georgia during the past twenty-five years, he has led projects to aid rural communities in planning and development, promote cultural conservation, and study the oral history and subcultures of the region.

CHRISTOPHER A. BROWN is the Social Marketing Specialist with the Bureau of Nutrition Services at the Texas Department of Health (Austin) and is responsible for coordinating statewide social marketing efforts of the Texas WIC Program. In 1992, he received his master's in applied anthropology from the University of South Florida (Tampa). He has worked on social marketing projects as a research analyst/project coordinator with Best Start Social Marketing (Tampa, Florida).

S. BRIDGET CIARAMITARO is the president of Ciaramitaro & Associates, Memphis, Tennessee, which she started in 1991. She received a master's from the University of Memphis in 1981. Her consulting business focuses on leadership development and empowerment of individuals, groups, businesses, and institutions in the Lower Mississippi Delta Region. She has several publications and was co-editor (with Shirley Fiske) of the July 1991 special issue of *Practicing Anthropology* on anthropology in the Mississippi Delta. She has received awards for her company's empowerment projects, including the 1995 Positive Images of Aging Award given by the Southeastern Association of Area Agencies on Aging (SE4A) for outstanding achievement in promoting positive and accurate images of aging.

MICHAEL M. ENGLISH has been the managing principal of the English Company, Inc., an urban planning consulting firm in Tampa, Florida, since 1989. He earned a master's in applied anthropology from the University of South Florida. A member of the Hillsborough County City-County Planning Commission since 1987, he is currently involved in the community's efforts to bring mass transit to the area, encourage the implementation of growth management in the area, and generally bring the anthropological perspective to the uninitiated in the Tampa area. He is a fellow of the Society for Applied Anthropology.

SUSAN EMLEY KEEFE is a professor and the chairperson of the Department of Anthropology at Appalachian State University (Boone, North Carolina). Her applied research interests have focused on ethnicity and ethnic relations and their impact on health and mental health, educational opportunity, and inequality. She has worked with Anglo-Americans, Mexican-Americans, and black and white Appalachian Americans. She is the author of *Chicano Ethnicity* (with Amado M. Padilla) and editor of *Appalachian Mental Health.*

MARY B. LA LONE is an associate professor of anthropology in the Department of Sociology and Anthropology at Radford University in Virginia. Her research has focused on economic anthropology and culture change in both historical and contemporary contexts in Andean Peru and Appalachian coal mining communities. She has presented and published numerous papers on the use and design of experiential learning projects for teaching anthropology.

SHARON GLICK MILLER is an assistant professor in the Department of Psychiatry at the University of South Florida in Tampa, Florida. She is the director of Family and Social Psychiatry and has conducted applied anthropological research on borderline personality disorder and recurrent diabetic ketoacidosis.

ANDREW W. MIRACLE is a professor of anthropology at Texas Christian University. He has authored or edited seven books on topics as diverse as sports, human sexuality, and language policy. Trained as an applied anthropologist, he has served as a consultant to a variety of educational, social service, and for-profit organizations.

ROBERT C. MORROW is an assistant professor of clinical pediatrics and assistant professor of clinical family and community medicine, Eastern Virginia Medical School of the Medical College of Hampton Roads. He was raised in Vermont, graduated Baylor College of Medicine in 1976, and earned a master's in public health at Harvard in 1975. In 1991, he completed the course work for a doctorate in sociomedical sciences at the University of Texas, Galveston. He is a fully trained pediatrician and his specialty is preventive medicine. In 1981 he was adopted into the Hunkpapa band of the Lakota Sioux, and in 1983 was a child specialist in the Kingdom of Bhutan. He is a member of the Baha'i Faith, and his main interest is culturally appropriate health care on American Indian Reservations and in Mongolia. He lives with his family in Norfolk, Virginia.

V. RICHARD PERSICO JR. is a professor of anthropology at Georgia Southern University and coordinator of the anthropology program. His research and teaching focus on the peoples and cultures of the American South including

Native Americans and European and African Americans. One of the central goals of his work is making anthropology accessible to the public.

SHANNON T. SCOTT is a 1995 bachelor's graduate of Radford University, Radford, Virginia, with a double major in anthropology and sociology. As an undergraduate student, she participated in projects that joined research in cultural anthropology with community service.

CHRISTOPHER P. TOUMEY received his doctorate at the University of North Carolina at Chapel Hill. He lives in Lexington, Kentucky, where he writes and teaches about the anthropology of science. His first book, *God's Own Scientists,* is an ethnography of the scientific creationist movement.

MELINDA BOLLAR WAGNER is a professor of anthropology and the associate chair of the Appalachian Studies Program at Radford University in Radford, Virginia. She has conducted research on both New Age and conservative Christian religions and is the author of *Metaphysics in Midwestern America* and *God's Schools: Choice and Compromise in American Society.* She has recently turned her attention to the study of cultural attachment to land, and to efforts at cultural conservation in the Appalachian region.

CHRISTOPHER H. WALKER is the documentation manager for BLAST, Inc., a communications software publisher. He has taught anthropology for the University of Maryland extension in Keflavík, Iceland, as well as for the University of North Carolina at Chapel Hill, where he received his doctorate. His research interests have included studying the symbolic aspects of faith healing among Pentecostals in the American South, from which resulted videotapes of several Pentecostal services, now housed in the University of North Carolina Non-Print collection. He also conducted a study of a black Pentecostal church network on the Caribbean island of Tobago. In addition, he has assisted Beverly Sizemore on a study of literacy and national identity in Iceland, the conclusions from which will be published in the upcoming volume, *Images of Contemporary Iceland.* He resides in Chapel Hill, North Carolina.

JAMES M. TIM WALLACE is an associate professor of anthropology in the Department of Sociology and Anthropology of North Carolina State University. His applied research includes community development and education in rural Peru, potato marketing in Ecuador, maize marketing in Mozambique, integrated pest management adoption among North Carolina farmers, food policy studies in the United States and Peru, and ecotourism in Madagascar.

He has been a consultant on projects for USAID, Sigma One Corporation, and the city of Keszthely, Hungary, among others. He is currently writing a book on sustainable development and tourism in the Balaton region of Hungary.

DANNY WOLFE is a registered nurse in a home health agency. A 1974 graduate of Radford University with a degree in English, he has taught school in Georgia and Virginia. In 1992, he returned to Radford University to pursue a degree in Appalachian Studies.

HONGGANG YANG teaches in the Master of Arts Program in Conflict Resolution (MACR) at the McGregor School of Antioch University. Before coming to the United States in 1986, he was on the faculty of social psychology and sociology at Nankai University in the People's Republic of China. He studied applied anthropology at the University of South Florida and was the 1989/1990 National Champion of the Scholarship Essay Competition for International Students. He received his doctorate in 1991. After graduation from the University of South Florida, he worked for the Conflict Resolution Program at the Carter Presidential Center. He is on the board of directors of the National Conference on Peacemaking and Conflict Resolution (NCPCR). His teaching and research interests include cross-cultural issues of conflict resolution, indigenous methods of dispute settlement, trust building, and management of the commons.